Gather 'Round the Table
with
Cee Dub
Dutch Oven
& Camp Cookin'

By C. W. "Butch" Welch

Back Country Press
Penny L. Welch, Publisher

Copyright © 2008 by C. W. "Butch" Welch

Printed in the United States of America
First Printing - 2008
Second Printing - 2013
Computer and Program Consultant - Gary Mitchell

ISBN # 978-0-9672647-0-7

DEDICATION

Every cook's career begins somewhere. Though it was years later when I learned that "KP" was army slang for "Kitchen Patrol", my cooking career began as KP duty when I was four or five years old. The "Kitchen Boss", Mom, would stand me on a stool in front of the kitchen sink to do lunch dishes while she did other chores. She was patient with my efforts until it came to drying the silverware. Having been a waitress before us kids came along, she knew a thing or two about how to get any kitchen chore done quickly. She would grab a whole handful of silverware along with a dish towel and head for the utensil drawer. She "very quickly" dried and placed each piece exactly where it belonged. This chore was done with all the slickness and finesse of a Las Vegas card shark dealing a hand of poker

Mom didn't realize it but she was ahead of her time in today's movement to prepare and serve healthier meals. On our one-acre lot, we had a big vegetable garden as well as growing all our own beef, pork, lamb, and poultry. Everything we raised was "organic" because having Dad and me clean our little barnyard put less strain on the family budget than buying commercial fertilizer. Mom canned and froze vegetables all summer long and in the fall bought fruit by the bushel to put up. Homemade jams, jellies, and pickles were stored in our basement's "fruit room". Emptied jars went back down to the fruit room for the next year's canning season. From these activities I learned the satisfaction to grow, harvest, and store my own food. To this day it gives me a great deal of satisfaction to put food on the table that originated as a product of my own labor.

Saturday was baking day at our old house on Hiway Avenue. During the school year Mom made enough bread for sack lunches for all four of us kids and Dad, as well as enough for toast and evening meals for the entire week. In grade school I remember feeling slighted because other kids had sandwiches made with store-bought Wonder Bread™. Little did I know how lucky I was!

Growing up, our kitchen was the most important room in the house. Why? Because we ate every meal together as a family! Every "Kitchen Boss" has his or her own sets of rules. Rule #1 at our house was that when Mom called out, "Supper's ready!", you had better get your hands washed pronto and get to the kitchen table! At the call, I'll always remember running in from outside and smelling dinner simmering on the stove, one of my favorites being Mom's Corned Beef and Dumplings! *

In high school it was a common occurrence for my buddy, Richard, and his little brother, Marc, to show up around supper time. Mom never complained or said a word about it; she just put out the additional place settings. One time "the extras" cut Mom a little short on quantities. Afterward, I apologized to her. She told me not to worry because she preferred to have my friends and me at home rather than worrying about where we were and what we were doing. Mom instilled in me how important it is for family and friends to "Gather 'Round the Table!"

Anyway,…Mom, I bet you never thought that little guy on the stool would go on to write five cookbooks and host TV cooking shows! So, Mom, "This cookbook is for YOU!"

*This favorite of Cee Dub's is included in this cookbook!

Table of Contents

ACKNOWLEDGEMENTS

How can words adequately thank everyone who contributed to this cookbook? Long after this old camp cook leaves this world and is sitting around the "Big Campfire in the Sky", future generations will reap the benefit of the contributions made by so many folks.

Any author knows the setting one chooses to write can make or break the end result. Without the generosity and hospitality of Dwain and Sandy Riney, owners of Las Piedras Ranch, I would have not experienced having my "perfect place" to research and write. The sense of peace one finds here at the end of a rough dirt road is priceless. Their son, Randy, also deserves credit for his contribution to my "Single Malt Cherry Pecan Rolls"!

Though many folks contributed to this cookbook, without the efforts of Gary Mitchell, our graphics guy, this project would just be another idea. Gary's willingness to teach and share his computer skills along with his selflessness in his time can't be adequately portrayed with mere words. He makes it all come together.

One of our themes in this book has been "sitting 'round the table". The time I've spent sitting around tables with our children, their spouses, and our grandchildren have truly provided inspiration to me. Extra special thanks go to Brian, Aaron and Ann, Matt and Trina, Abigail, Alec, Anna, Wyatt, and Maggie.

Without the help of my brother in-law, Al Kusy, who runs www.ceedubs.com , does our product fulfillment, and runs our customer service department, I would forever be swimming upstream!

Though most folks call her Pen or Penny, she also answers to Mom and Grandma; but around here she goes by "Babe"! Someone once asked Babe what she was paid for slicing, dicing, doing dishes, acting as in-house counsel, editing, typing, photography, etc., etc. Without batting an eye she replied, "Three and a half a day...three meals and half a bed!" About the only way I see to give you a raise, Babe, is to start cooking a fourth meal everyday! All my love, Babe!

FOREWARD

Over the past twenty-five years, I've been fortunate to see some amazing places, do some amazing things, and eat countless savory meals prepared by Cee Dub, although I simply refer to him as "Dad." As anyone who knows my dad will tell you, the food is only half of the experience. The stories and subsequent laughter are the other constant and always prove to be as memorable as the food.

Whether we were at the house in Grangeville, Idaho, or Las Piedras Ranch in Texas, family dinners have always been relatively simple but always special. In the summer, Dad always had the charcoal grill out for some Brats, Polish, or German Sausages. Thanksgiving dinners usually meant a wild turkey cooked in a turkey roaster. However, still one of my favorite memories as a kid was Elk hunting on Thanksgiving Day in the Bitterroot Mountains. One particular year it was snowing sideways, and my dad and I found refuge under a tree and had ham sandwiches and candy bars. Quick and easy at its best!

I've been lucky enough to taste all of my dad's more intricate dishes such as Chicken Cacciatore, but my favorite meals were the most simple. As far as I'm concerned, nothing beats the "standard breakfast" consisting of sausage, eggs, and fried potatoes after a long morning of hunting.

Brian guiding on Salmon River   Summer 2005
                                                 B Welch Photo

Brian rafting on MF Salmon River   Summer 2008
                                                B Welch Photo

My dad's knowledge in all things outdoors and cooking is quite extensive, and I have learned a lot from him. At first, I thought outdoor cooking would be genetic, but I found that to be wrong (as an unnamed Fire Department in Northern Idaho can attest)! However, I have turned out to be a decent outdoor cook and all the credit goes to my dad.

I cannot talk about my dad's cooking without also talking about my stepmom, Penny. Any meal, whether at home, camp, or a cooking show, is always a team effort between my dad and Penny. They truly enjoy each other's company and working together. The food is always delicious, and time spent with them is truly a blessing.

I know Dad and Penny had a great time creating this cookbook because outdoor cooking is their lifestyle. They would encourage beginners and experienced cooks alike to experiment and have fun with the recipes in this cookbook. Having fun is the essence of outdoor cooking and all of Cee Dub's Cookbooks – good friends, great food, and memorable stories to last a lifetime. Enjoy!

Brian Welch
November 2008
Boise, Idaho

AUTHOR'S NOTE

When Pen and I started kicking around ideas for a new cookbook, a chance remark made by a good friend and former Dutch oven student, Ray Shaeffer, at a Texas steakhouse started us thinking. A bunch of us, all graying and balding baby boomers, were sitting at a big round table enjoying the National Dish of Texas, i.e., chicken fried steak, and talking about the "good ol' days"! Ray had an epiphany that ultimately helped Pen and I choose the direction for this cookbook. He made the statement that in the 1960's he wore "bell bottom pants"; and now he is wearing "bell bottom shirts"! In my own case, I wore the same size jeans for the first thirty years after high school graduation; but, as my fortieth reunion approaches, I admit seeing my belt buckle takes a little extra effort.

Then a year or so ago Pen and I were at Don and Kris Van Cleave's house, long time friends of ours, sitting around the table drinking malted beverages while a couple of Dutch ovens simmered out on their back patio. At some point the conversation turned to how much of our lives and many of our best memories center around gatherings of family and friends at the breakfast or supper table. Once we started on the subject we went on for hours. It was sometime after midnight that Don broke out a family photo album to show us pictures of the huge cedar plank table in their vacation cabin on a lake in British Columbia. What struck me even at that late hour was the numbers of celebrations witnessed by the old chunk of cedar. There were birthdays, anniversaries, winning the family's annual 'big fish' contest, and other memorable family events all celebrated at the table. Don even said that the table had helped raise their two sons and the pictures proved it. There were pictures of Kyle and Kelly as toddlers, through their teens, and as handsome adult young men. Don suggested that we somehow incorporate this theme in the title and throughout the next cookbook.

As we've traveled around the last few years, lots of folks have asked us about not only cooking "lighter" but also for recipes that will fit in eight or ten inch Dutch ovens. Many of our generation are now empty nesters. Their kids have all grown and left home, and cooking for two turns out to be more of a challenge than keeping up with a whole bunch of hungry kids. As you work your way through this cookbook, you'll see how we've focused our efforts toward a healthier style of Dutch oven cookin'. Many of the recipes we've chosen are "lighter" recipes, we've including sources for obtaining nutritional information, and we've provided instructions on "down-sizing" your favorite recipes as well. But like anyone who enjoys a variety of dishes, we have included a few "gut busters" as well.

I hope you enjoy this cookbook and have as much fun using it as we did in researching and writing it!

Cee Dub
Las Piedras Ranch
Real County, Texas
Fall 2008

GATHER 'ROUND THE TABLE

     I'm sure a study exists somewhere detailing how much time the average person spends sitting at a table eating. It's my guess, though, no such study exists that quantifies the good times and sad times we all experience sitting around the dining room table with family and friends! It's been my privilege to sit at dining room tables that cost more than I make in a year, and I've also eaten many suppers using nothing more than an old tree stump for a table in hunting camp. Call it personal preference, but I'll choose flickering firelight instead of candle light for ambiance any day. So, for my money it doesn't matter if it's a polished family heirloom, the tailgate of a truck, a Roll-A-Table™ on a sandy beach, or a corner booth in an out of the way Texas steakhouse; sharing a meal with family and friends ranks close to the top of what is great about life.

     It seems, though, that as the pace of society increases, the amount of time spent as families at the

Cheers to a mouth-watering prime rib dinner at *LPR 2007*
Welch Photo Collection

supper table decreases. If I could magically reverse just the part about sitting around the dinner table, I suspect it wouldn't cure all that's wrong in the world, but I do believe it would help a little bit. Just sorting through our family photos for this cookbook brought back many memories and resulted in the re-telling of lots of stories.

It's been said that a person shouldn't drink alone, and I believe that goes as well for eating alone. Even just one other person sitting across the table sharing a meal and conversation beats eating solo.

Call me old fashioned, but I don't see much quality family time involved with fast food and microwave meals. I guess that is why I enjoy my Dutch ovens. I use the time while my Dutch ovens and wood coals work their magic to visit with whoever is in the kitchen, whether I'm at home or in camp. Regardless of the trials and tribulations the day may have thrown at us, folks gathered around the table seem to forget those daily events for awhile when the lids come off the pots! So, enjoy this cookbook, and while waiting for something to cook sometime, take a few minutes to sort through some of your old pictures of friends and family gathered 'round the table.

ABOUT THE COVERS

In late 2006, Pen and I moved from North Central Idaho to the Texas Hill Country. It was a big change, but change is good! When we set the tent up on the toe of a small ridge just above the Las Piedras Ranch ranch house, we thought we'd be calling it home for a short time until we found our own place. But over time, we find ourselves living at, and managing, the ranch. More than a few of the recipes in this cookbook were first served and tested on guests here at LPR. It took some doing to get the cover photo. The ground drops away very fast in front of the tent. The only way Pen could get high enough to snap the photo was to stand on a load of hay on "Dynamite," the 1968 Ford ¾ ton flatbed ranch truck. And let's not talk about how long it took to get the perfect pose of Rosie and Scooter!

During the summer of 2006, Bryant Truitt of Hunt, Texas, spoke with Pen in Idaho to inquire about our Dutch Oven University. She told him we were fixin' to move to the Texas Hill Country in just a few months. Bryant and his wife, Shari, have become dear friends. Some months after we moved to Texas, Bryant met us at a sports show in Redmond, Oregon. Along with witnessing first hand the "Herb, Hobie, and Cee Dub" show in the Camp Cooking Demonstration Tent, he snapped some pictures of Cee Dub doing his "Hillbilly Cookin'" demonstration. One of those pictures we chose for the back cover. Many thanks to Bryant!

Cee Dub and Bryant Truitt at a Dutch oven clinic in Hunt, Texas - 2006   Triutt Photo Collection

UP-SIZING, DOWN-SIZING & CONVERTING RECIPES

Dutch ovens are like a lot of other things in life, one size doesn't fit all. The 12" DO tends to be considered the standard size and is the most popular. The occasions occur when folks want to convert a recipe from their home kitchen to a Dutch oven as well as increasing or decreasing the size of a recipe. Just using a little common sense when it comes to increasing or decreasing the size of a recipe is much easier than generating a complicated series of mathematic equations to precisely determine how to up-size or down-size recipes.

As a general rule I use the volumetric capacity of the ovens in question as a best guess on how to change amounts necessary to use the recipe in a different size DO. For example, a 12" DO has a capacity of six quarts, and a 10" DO holds four quarts. To down-size a recipe from a 12" oven to a 10" oven will require cutting the recipe by about a third. When changing Dutch oven sizes, keep in mind that your recipe should have about an inch between the top of the food and the lid. There is a tendency to overfill a smaller oven because the ingredients weren't reduced sufficiently. The reverse pretty well holds true when increasing the size of a recipe for a larger Dutch oven.

Converting recipes from your home kitchen for use in a Dutch oven is very easy as well. A standard 9 x 13 inch casserole dish or baking pan has the same volume as a 12" DO. That makes it easy to convert many home recipes for your Dutch oven. Similarly, a 9 x 9 inch baking dish has about the same volume as a 10" DO. Just prepare the recipes with the same ingredients for your DO's as you would at home. By the same token favorite camp dishes made in 10" and 12" DO's can easily be made at home.

In summary, just use your head and a calculator to convert your recipes to other sizes.

Appetizers

Bruschetta **

Ingredients:

1 French baguette, cut into ½ inch circles
3 Tbsp. olive oil
2 cloves garlic, minced or pressed
4 Roma tomatoes, diced
1 cup chopped fresh basil
½ red onion, minced
Fresh ground black pepper
¾ cup grated mozzarella cheese

Preheat oven to 400 degrees. Arrange bread circles on a baking sheet. Bake in oven until well toasted, approximately 5 minutes. Remove bread from oven. In a small bowl, mix olive oil and garlic. Brush bread circles with olive oil and garlic mixture. Combine tomatoes, basil, and red onion in a small bowl; season with black pepper. Spoon the tomato mixture generously onto each circle. Sprinkle cheese on each slice. Place bread circles on a large serving platter and serve. Serves 14 to 16.

Trina Dykas
Boise, Idaho

** A photo of this recipe is featured at the beginning of the "Appetizers and Snacks" section.

Words of Wisdom

To prevent the mess in making cracker or bread crumbs, first place crackers in plastic bag and then roll with a rolling pin.

When camping with kids, always pack a separate cooler with their snacks and drinks. It keeps them out of the cook's hair

—— Cinnamon and Sugar Chips ——

Ingredients:

1 tsp. cinnamon
2 tsp. sugar
8 flour tortillas, 8-inch size
Vegetable oil, for frying

In a small bowl, stir the cinnamon and sugar together; set aside. Cut each tortilla into six wedges. In a large, deep skillet, or 12 inch Dutch oven, heat about one inch of oil over medium heat until it shimmers. While heating the oil, cover a plate with several layers of paper towels. In batches, place the tortilla wedges into the oil and fry for about 30 seconds per side, or until golden brown. Transfer the browned chips onto the paper towels and let them drain for 20 to 30 seconds. Place still warm chips in a brown paper bag or reclosable plastic bag. Add several pinches of the cinnamon and sugar mix, then close the bag and gently shake to coat the chips. Pour the chips onto a serving plate and repeat with remaining ingredients. Serve with Cinnamon Chip Dip, in this section.

Betty Welch
Pocatello, Idaho

—— Cinnamon and Sugar Chip Dip ——

Ingredients:

4 oz. cream cheese
6 oz. vanilla yogurt
4 tsp. sugar
½ tsp. cinnamon

In a small mixing bowl, beat all the ingredients together until smooth. Serve with Cinnamon and Sugar Chips, recipe above in this section.

Cleavers' Hot Brats

We made this recipe as an appetizer for an event at the Van Cleaves' famous barn. The Van Cleaves carry the nickname of "Cleavers"; hence, the name of the recipe. It turned out to be a favorite for get-togethers, river trips, birthday parties, and holidays. One thing we learned, though, is that if you make this recipe, you had better plan on at least doubling or tripling the recipe!

Ingredients:

1 lb. bratwurst
¼ cup Hoisin sauce
¼ cup hot sauce
2 Tbsp. orange marmalade
2 cloves garlic, minced
1 tsp. grated ginger
½ tsp. chili powder
½ tsp. ground cumin
½ tsp. dry mustard
1 Tbsp. chopped cilantro
1 tsp. sesame seeds

Preheat grill to medium heat. Sear the brats. Reduce heat to low and continue to grill brats for 25 to 30 minutes until done. Remove brats and allow to cool. Cut brats into 1 inch, bite-size pieces. Combine sauce ingredients in a bowl. Put the sliced brats into the sauce and mix, thoroughly coating all the brat pieces. Place coated brat pieces back on the grill and cook for a few more minutes, turning as needed, to heat thoroughly. Remove from heat and serve. Serves 4 to 6.

Cee Dub & Penny Welch
Mountain Home, Texas

═ THREE GUYS IN THE KITCHEN ═
aka
The Herb, Hobie, & Cee Dub Show

Cooking is supposed be fun but nothing I've ever done prepared me for the fun in my future with a couple of fellow camp cooks, Herb Good and Hobart Manns. I'd been hired two months earlier by O'Loughlin Trade Shows of Portland, Oregon, to do Dutch oven cooking demonstrations at their four Northwest sportsmen's shows.

Even with several years of experience doing cooking demos I had a bad case of pre-game jitters when we pulled up to the Camp Cooking Demonstration tent to unload. I knew Herb Good and Hobart Manns had done these shows together for about ten years. The third cook who had been doing the shows for several years had dropped out and I was going to be the new kid on the block. Herb and Hobart, aka Hobie were already in the tent unloading their gear. Both were cordial and professional when we first met. To this day Hobie is always courteous and professional; but I confess it took Herb just overnight to start showing me a different side.

The first day of a show always ends up being a bit hectic and it was even more so for Pen, and me. Though way too big to be mistaken for a leprechaun Herb's mischievous side soon started showing. We were all scurrying around working on last minute projects before the show opened. Herb would wait until I was focused on something then holler, "CEE DUB, WHAT TIME IS IT?". Of course I would quickly check my watch and go back to what I'd been doing as Herb chuckled for anyone with in earshot. Minutes later it would be, "CEE DUB, LOOK AT YOUR WATCH!", followed by more laughter. Though good natured I knew it was just part of the test to see how thick my skin was. (Not to worry though, twenty-one years as a game warden had thickened my hide substantially!)

From a professional perspective I quickly realized how good both these guys were in a camp kitchen. Hobie though long retired from his day job has hunted, fished, and traipsed around the Northwest for over half a century. In addition he does some outdoor writing and has a radio show in his home town of Portland, Oregon. Herb is semi retired from forty plus years as a fishing guide. For sixteen years he and another guy had a fishing camp on Alaska's Kenai River. In addition he spent time in Russia guiding fishermen after the end of the Cold War. Watching them both breeze through their presentations those first couple of days caused my jitters to continue as we worked to adjust to the new venue and format.

Never before had I shared a kitchen like this. At other venues where I was the only demonstrator it didn't matter if my demo ran a bit long. Not here! With a different demonstrator every hour on the hour we had to prep, cook, serve, and clean up in an hour. Pen and I are fast learners but we had our work cut out for us. Both Herb and Hobie cut us some slack those first few days which helped us make the transition! However....

Besides the black felt cowboy hat he always wears, his size, lack of Irish ancestry, Herb cannot claim leprechaun status. But trust me, beneath that black cowboy hat resides a spirit to make any leprechaun proud!!! It started about day two in a discussion over sharing refrigerator space. There are two fridges in the prep area with one being for Herb's use while Hobie and I share the other. Herb's idea of sharing is that as soon as his fridge is full he brings his overflow over and shares with Hobie and me. Herb in a serious tone of voice told me it best if I wrote my name on our groceries to eliminate mix ups. (I didn't mention that neither he nor Hobie had labeled their groceries.) After he walked away, I walked outside to see if there was a turnip truck parked there that I'd fallen off of and just couldn't remember. There wasn't!

Both semi retired fishing guides and old game wardens tend to get up early in the morning and sometimes it's just a matter of who gets up first. So, the next morning I made damn sure I beat Herb to the kitchen. I had my head down slicing and dicing when Herb waltzed in after a night of burning up shoe leather on a couple of local dance floors. (Though you might have trouble painting a mental image of Herb as an accomplished dancer, trust me, he is in great demand!) Anyway…Herb continued humming some ballroom music as he washed his hands and put on an apron. The music stopped when he opened the door on his fridge and saw "CEE DUB" written on everything in it including the five dozen eggs for his famous "Cabbage Omelet". Hobie, always the consummate straight man, merely turned away silently laughing!

As in days of old, Herb had thrown down the gauntlet and I picked it up accepting the challenge of a duel that continues to this day! Though Herb is a wee bit older than I we both have a lot in common. (So much in common that some folks think I'm his little brother which really causes Herb heartburn!) Among those things we have in common is we both subscribe to the philosophy of "Don't get mad, get even, and then get ahead!" It didn't take Herb long at all!

Instead of wearing a wrist watch, I've always preferred a pocket watch. So, when I get to the kitchen, I set it on the corner of my prep table so I can glance at it as I help Pen do the morning prep work. It was Sunday morning and I was first on the schedule. Being focused on making this last day of the show a good one I was extra busy. As I recall the doors opened at 10:00 A.M. and my first demo was scheduled for 10:30 A.M. No matter how fast I worked every time I glanced at my watch I had more to do and less time to do it. Time was flying. As 10:30 A.M. approached I still had 15-20 minutes of prep to do. With less than five minutes to go I hit the panic button. With not a single spectator in the tent, I huffed up and said, "I'm not going to do a demo if no one is here!" Hobie's wife, Meiri, who assists him gave it away when she looked at her watch and said, "Cee Dub, the doors are just now opening, it's only 10:00 A.M., you have plenty of time"! Then the laughter started! While I was scurrying around getting ready, an oversized leprechaun imitator wearing a black cowboy hat had been setting my watch ahead five minutes every time I turned my back. There was nothing to do but heave a sigh of relief and laugh along!

One of our traditions at these shows is to cook for the others. Besides being in a time crunch most of the day our cooking is better than what the food vendors usually have. One morning while working on his third helping of my "Baked Oatmeal" Herb sarcastically said he'd rather be hit in the face with a dirty diaper than eat my cooking. Oh really I thought to myself! Again the old game warden got up earlier than the semi retired fishing guide. I was at the grocery store in the grey light of dawn getting grub for the day but I made sure to include on my list some disposable diapers, extra crunchy peanut butter, yellow mustard, and a can of Mountain Dew™. When Herb found a dirty diaper front and center on his prep table he knew that he'd given me the idea himself and it was his turn to laugh along with the rest of us!

With our fifth year doing these shows about to start I must say the "duel" between Herb and me lives on along with lots of silent laughter from Hobie! Besides having a great friendship with Hobie, his wife Meiri, and Herb; all three of them have been very gracious in sharing some of their recipes for this book. Between the three of us we count well over a hundred years of camp cooking experience. Hobie and Meiri shared their slice of heaven on Brownlee Reservoir when they hosted us for a crappie fishing trip. Pen caught her first steelhead while fishing with Herb. Being the new kid on the block has been a great adventure and a fantastic opportunity to learn from two of the best camp cooks anywhere!

Besides saying thanks to the folks at O'Loughlin Trade Shows for making the Hobie, Herb, & Cee Dub show possible I need to thank two others as well. Jack Smith, Herb's long time fishing partner and sometimes kitchen assistant provides much needed dead pan humor and agrees with those who think Herb and I look like brothers. Lastly I need to mention Hook! Along with accompanying Herb on countless hunting and fishing trips, Hook, a classy Black Lab, tagged along with Herb on his cooking gigs. He knew his place in the kitchen and was friendly to everyone. Hook went to the "Great Duck Blind in the Sky" during the Portland Sport Show in 2005. We miss you, Hook!

Herb, one of the three guys in the kitchen '08

Hobart (and his wife & assistant, Meiri) , ... another guy in the kitchen '08

Welch Photo Collection

Words of Wisdom

Learn to make simple sauces and dressings from supplies you already have in camp. It will save money at the grocery store, plus you will have fresher and healthier condiments. You can customize your recipes, too, by making your own. See examples of easy recipes in this cookbook.

Easy Quesadillas

Ingredients:

Precooked sausage, chopped
Green pepper, chopped
Red pepper, chopped
White or green onions, chopped
Mushrooms, chopped
Favorite cheese, grated
Hot sauce, if desired
Flour tortillas
Sour cream
Salsa

Preheat the lid of a 10 inch Dutch oven; and preheat the DO using 6 briquets under the oven. Place a tortilla in the bottom of the DO. Sprinkle some meat and chopped vegetables over the tort; then sprinkle cheese on top. Add a few drops of hot sauce, if desired. Place another tort on top. Cover with the hot DO lid. Heat until cheese melts. Remove quesadilla onto plate and cut into wedges. Serve with sour cream and salsa. While eating that quesadilla, have another one heating. Great in camp for an appetizer or quick snack. Note: The vegetables and meat can all be sautéed ahead of time, if desired, before placing on torts.

—— Pen's Roasted Pumpkin Seeds ——

I stumbled on making this treat several years ago. Now Butch anxiously brings home several pumpkins each Halloween season so that we can enjoy the seeds as well as the Jack-O-Lanterns that he enjoys carving.

Ingredients:

2 cups seeds, cleaned
½ stick butter, melted
2 tsp. cumin
1 tsp. salt

Place all ingredients in a bowl and mix thoroughly until all seeds are coated. Pour out onto a cookie sheet and spread evenly. Bake at 250 degrees for 45 to 50 minutes. Stir them around a couple of times so they brown evenly. Increase heat to 300 and continue baking for an additional 15 minutes.

Penny Welch
Mountain Home, Texas

Jack-O-Lanterns and Ghosts at the Welch house on Halloween

Welch Photo
        Collection

30

Herb demonstrating how to filet a salmon in Monroe, Washington 2008   Welch Photo Collection

———— Salmon Cookies ————

Ingredients:

1 can pink or red salmon
¼ lb. crackers, rolled
1 egg
Chopped veggies, such as onions, green onions,
     jalapenos, celery, as desired
Salt, pepper, and seasonings to taste

Mix all ingredients together in a bowl. With fingers, form balls and flatten into cookie-shaped patties; or, can make larger patties for sandwiches. Fry and brown in hot oil in a skillet. Put on paper towel to drain and cool. Serve plain or with Quick Tartar Sauce for a dip or sandwich spread.

Herb Good
Hood River, Oregon

Jon Greco and Cee Dub on horse patrol in downtown Chicago   Welch Photo Collection

Walking Tacos

Our friend, Jon Greco, said, "This is a dish that Sue and I have served up to our kids and their families from St. John Fisher Parish/School in Chicago at Football, Soccer, and Volleyball games. I think that it would go well at camp, tailgating, and other outdoor events...."

Ingredients:

2 lbs. ground beef (Sue says that will feed
        20 to 30 folks)
2 pkg. taco or chili seasoning mix
2 cans beans
1-2 medium yellow onions, chopped
1 green pepper, chopped; or
        hot peppers, if desired
Other desired spices or seasonings
20-30 pkg. lunch-box size Fritos™ or
        Doritos™ corn chips
Condiments... such as lettuce, tomatoes,
        cheese, salsa, sour cream
Plastic spoons or forks

Brown ground beef in a Dutch oven and mix in packages of seasoning mix. Add beans, onions, peppers, and other spices. Scoop a large spoonful of meat mixture into the bag of chips. Add condiments and a plastic spoon or fork.

"That's it…no muss, no fuss!"

Jon added, "Now, this got me to thinking that you could probably do such things as 'Walking Pizza' using small bags of potato chips, red sauce, peppers, onions, mushrooms, and cheese…

or; how about the 'Walking U-Boat' using chips, bulk German sausage cooked with sauerkraut and topped with cheese…or the 'Walking Polka' with chips, bulk Polish sausage cooked with sauerkraut and onions…just thinking!"

Jon and Sue Greco
Chicago, Illinois

—— Jicama and Orange Salsa ——

Ingredients:

6 oranges, peeled, sectioned, and chopped
2 cups peeled, cubed jicama
2 green onions, chopped
1/3 cup chopped purple onion
1/3 cup chopped red pepper
1/3 cup minced cilantro
1/3 cup chopped Roma tomatoes
½ tsp. minced garlic, if desired
1 Tbsp. lime juice
2 tsp. seeded, chopped jalapeno peppers,
          more or less to taste
1/4 tsp. salt
1/2 tsp. sugar

Combine all ingredients in a large bowl and chill. Serve with tortilla chips or scoops. Makes 4 to 5 cups.

Sautéed Shrimp and
──────── Artichokes ────────

Ingredients:

1 lb. raw medium shrimp, peeled, rinsed,
    and deveined
2 Tbsp. butter
2 Tbsp. olive oil
2 cloves garlic, minced
4 green onions, coarsely chopped
½ lb. fresh mushrooms, coarsely chopped
1 16 oz. can artichoke hearts,
    drained and sliced in half
2 Tbsp. vinegar
2 Tbsp. lemon juice
½ tsp. dried oregano
½ tsp. salt
Freshly ground pepper, to taste

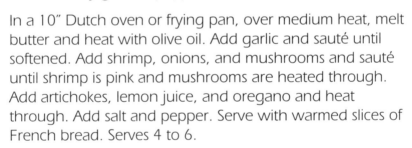

In a 10" Dutch oven or frying pan, over medium heat, melt butter and heat with olive oil. Add garlic and sauté until softened. Add shrimp, onions, and mushrooms and sauté until shrimp is pink and mushrooms are heated through. Add artichokes, lemon juice, and oregano and heat through. Add salt and pepper. Serve with warmed slices of French bread. Serves 4 to 6.

Rick Carrico
Twin Falls, Idaho

──── Words of Wisdom ────

To clean and restore the color of your plastic ice chests, use oven cleaner. After spraying the cooler with the oven cleaner, let it sit for 2 to 3 minutes; then scrub with a stiff bristle brush. Rinse with cold water.

Sugared Pecans

Ingredients:

1 lb. pecan halves
1 egg white
1 Tbsp. water
1 cup sugar
1 tsp. salt
1 tsp. cinnamon

Preheat oven to 300 degrees. Beat egg white with water into a froth. In a large resealable bag, combine sugar, salt, and cinnamon. Dip pecans in the egg white. Place coated pecans in the bag containing the sugar mixture and shake, coating them well. Place on a cookie sheet coated with oil or non-stick spray. Bake for 40 minutes, or until egg white is dry. Stir every ten minutes. Cool on waxed paper. This treat is yummy on ice cream; and, it freezes well.

Yummy Hummus

Ingredients:

2 cloves garlic
1 15 oz. can garbanzo beans, or chickpeas,
        rinsed and drained
¼ cup lemon juice
3 Tbsp. water
2 Tbsp. tahini*
1 tsp. cumin
¼ tsp. salt
¼ tsp. pepper

Process all ingredients in a food processor until smooth. Transfer to a small bowl. Makes about 1 ½ cups. Serve with pita bread wedges or use as a vegetable dip.

*Tahini is a paste made from ground sesame seeds. If the seeds have been hulled, the flavor is mild, whereas unhulled seeds may result in a slightly bitter taste. Tahini is found in the ethnic section of most grocery stores.

Breads

Egg Noodles drying for soup and lasagna at Ranch Clinic
May 2008   Dave Horner Photo

Egg Noodles

Ingredients:

3 egg yolks
1 whole egg
Splash of cold water, about 2 Tbsp.
Pinch of salt
2 cups flour

Put egg yolks and whole egg in a bowl. Add the splash
of cold water and salt. Beat the eggs with a fork. Start
adding flour, small amounts at a time, and mix with the
eggs. Continue adding flour and mixing until dough forms
a stiff ball and is not sticky. Turn dough out onto a floured
board. Begin kneading dough, adding small amounts
of flour while working dough. Continue kneading until
dough is no longer sticky, but is stiff. Work dough into a
ball and let it rest for about 15 minutes. Divide dough into
two to four parts. Roll each piece out on a floured board
until very thin. If making lasagna noodles, roll out thicker.
Lay out sheets of newspaper and cover with wax paper.
Let noodles dry until ends begin to curl. Fold up and cut
into desired size of noodles. If making lasagna noodles, cut
into desired width with pizza cutter or vegetable cutter.
Spread noodles out on a cookie sheet to dry. Noodles can
be frozen for use later.

Al assisting Cee Dub at a store demonstration August 2008
Welch Photo Collection

Al's No Knead
——— Dutch Oven Bread ** ———

Ingredients:

3 cups all-purpose flour, white, whole wheat, or
 a combination
½ tsp. active dry yeast
1 ½ tsp. salt
1 ¾ cups warm water
Cornmeal, flour, or wheat bran for dusting

In a large bowl, put in the flour, yeast, and salt; mix
together thoroughly. Add the water and thoroughly mix
with hand until dough is consistent. The dough will be
shaggy and sticky. Cover bowl with plastic wrap. Let the
dough rest at least 12 to 18 hours, at room temperature,
about 70 degrees. The dough is ready when its surface
is dotted with bubbles. Lightly flour a work surface with
flour, cornmeal, or bran; and, place dough on flour.
Sprinkle the dough with a little more flour and fold it over

on itself twice, like a letter. Turn it over onto the folds. Cover loosely with plastic wrap and let it rest for about 15 minutes. At least 20 minutes before the dough is ready, preheat oven to 500 degrees. Put a 10" Dutch oven in the oven as it heats. Leave the lid off, but in the oven. When the dough is ready, carefully slide the oven rack out so that you have access to the DO. Slide your hand under the dough and turn the dough over and into the pot, seam side up. The dough will lose its shape a bit in the process. Cover with the lid and bake for 30 minutes. Remove the lid and bake another 5 to 8 minutes, until the loaf is beautifully browned. Remove the bread from the DO and let it cool on a rack for at least 1 hour before slicing. NOTES: Al has used 1 cup whole wheat flour in place of 1 cup unbleached flour and he states it was fantastic. Also, use heavy gloves because of the 500 degree temperatures.

Al Kusy
Meridian, Idaho

** A photo of this recipe is featured at the beginning of the "Breads" section.

Uncle Al giving Wyatt his first piano lesson August 2008
Welch Photo Collection

—— Cee Dub's Easy Dinner Rolls ——

Being somewhat of a purist when it came to baking in Dutch ovens, I used to always make bread and rolls from scratch, starting most often by removing my sourdough starter from the refrigerator, letting it come to room temperature, and feeding it. Anyone that bakes using sourdough knows that it can become a labor of love and time intensive.

However, most everyone we teach in our classes wants to learn how to bake biscuits, bread, or rolls in that new Dutch oven received as a gift from a friend or family.

I never thought I would come to rely on doing things the easy way, but when teaching folks about baking in Dutch ovens, I have learned that teaching how to **bake** bread and rolls, rather than how to **make** bread and rolls, yields greater success with students.

Doing things the easy way also enables us to bake rolls within the time constraints of scheduled demonstrations and events. The following recipe is not only easy and a confidence builder, but also will bring out rave reviews at the table and requests for more.

Ingredients:

1 pkg., 24 Texas or 36 count, Rhodes™ frozen
      dinner rolls
1 stick butter
1 cup seasoned bread crumbs

Thaw rolls. Melt butter in a small pan or 5" Dutch oven. Place bread crumbs in another container. Roll each roll first in melted butter, then in bread crumbs. Place rolls evenly in bottom of a 16" Dutch oven. Allow rolls to rise until doubled in size. Cover DO and bake rolls at 350 to 375 for 15 to 20 minutes using 12-14 briquets under the oven and 35-40 briquets on the lid, until golden brown. Turn out on a board when hot to cool. Serve warm.

Cee Dub making his Easy Dinner Rolls at a store demo
August 2008   Welch Photo Collection

Flour Tortillas

Ingredients:

6 cups flour
1 ½ tsp. salt
2 tsp. baking powder
1 tsp. baking soda
1 tsp. lard

In a bowl mix all ingredients working into a crumbly dough, similar to texture of Bisquick™. Add water to make dough stick together, coming off the side of the bowl. Place dough on a floured board and knead the he&% out of it. Let it rest covered for about 20 minutes. Knead some more; dough is tough and hard to work. To make a tortilla about 8 inches, pull off a piece of dough the size of a golf ball. Use a rolling pin to roll out to desired thickness. Makes 20 to 24 tortillas. NOTE: Using a tortilla press to form the torts takes out much of the hard work and time.

Dave and Denise Carmichael
Emmett, Idaho

Exotic critters decked out for
Christmas '08 Welch Photos

Eggnog Muffins

Ingredients:

3 cups flour
½ cup sugar
3 tsp. baking powder
½ tsp. salt
½ tsp. ground nutmeg
1 egg
1 ¾ cups commercial eggnog
½ cup vegetable oil
½ cup golden raisins
½ cup chopped pecans

In a large bowl, combine flour, sugar, baking powder, salt and nutmeg. In another bowl, combine the egg, eggnog, and oil; stir into dry ingredients just until moistened. Fold in raisins and pecans. Fill greased or paper-lined muffin cups two-thirds full. Bake at 350 degrees for 20 to 25 minutes or until a toothpick comes out clean. Cool for 5 minutes before removing from pans to a wire rack. Makes 16 muffins.

SOURDOUGH

History:

My first memory of the term "sourdough" dates back to my childhood reading articles in Sports Afield by Ted Trueblood when Dad and I made our regular Saturday morning trip to the barber shop. Along about the same time a grade school assignment was to read Jack London's classic, *The Call of the Wild*, set in the Klondike gold rush of the late 1890's. My first experience of sourdough, though, was when a college buddy introduced me to sourdough pancakes at a hunting camp in the early 1970's. The taste hooked me with the very first forkful, and I soon began tinkering with sourdough cooking myself. More years than I care to remember elapsed before my tinkering changed to intrigue and I began to research "sourdough".

The first thing my research showed was sourdough did not originate during the Klondike gold rush, but actually has a history dating back at least 5000 years. Archeological evidence in Egypt from around 3000 B.C. indicates breads leavened with wild yeasts were a staple of workers constructing the pyramids during ancient times. Until commercial bakers' yeast first became available in the late 1800's, all yeast leavened breads around the world were made with a "sourdough" culture.

As is typical as when something new comes along, like commercial bakers' yeast, the "old fashioned" way of doing things began to disappear. Though the familiar bakers' yeast we buy in the grocery store is what most home bakers use, sourdough cultures are still used today by folks around the world. However, the love affair Alaskan's have had with sourdough since those early gold rush days continues to the present; and, I believe is largely responsible for keeping the art of sourdough cooking alive and well.

Definitions:

"Sourdough" - fermenting dough: fermenting dough used as a leavening agent in making bread. (Encarta ® World English Dictionary)

In more specific terms, a sourdough culture contains strains of "wild yeast" for leavening the bread and bacteria called *Lacto bacilli sp.* which gives bread leavened in this manner their characteristic "sour" flavor. The metabolic byproducts of yeast are carbon dioxide which leavens the bread, i.e., causes it to rise, and alcohol. Lactic acid actually gives the bread its characteristic sour taste and is a metabolic by product of *Lacto bacilli sp.*

Starter – A mixture of flour, water, wild yeast and *Lacto bacilli sp.* (Some authors refer to starter and culture interchangeably; however I prefer to use the term starter.)

First Proof - "Feeding the starter a 1:1 ratio of water to flour, and allowing it to sit in a warm environment. This allows the dormant yeast and bacteria to rejuvenate and activate.

Sponge – An activated starter that has been fed a 1:1 mixture of water to flour. This activated starter is the basic building block for all sourdough breads and recipes.

Hooch - The liquid that rises to the top when the starter or sponge has utilized all the nutrients after it has been fed or activated. The hooch contains alcohol but with exposure to air converts to weak vinegar. Do not pour the hooch off; just stir it back into the starter.

Second Proof - After adding other ingredients to the sponge as called for in any given recipe for bread, when the bread is allowed to rise prior to baking.

Where do I get a Starter?

There are three different ways to obtain a starter. My favorite source of sourdough starters is to get one from someone who has a starter. Often these starters will have been handed down through a family for several generations. I don't know that a starter's history or pedigree makes the final product taste any better, but it makes for great conversation while in the kitchen or camp. In addition to commercially available starters, it is actually quite easy to start your very own starter.

Starting your own starter

Here are the two methods I've personally used to start starters. Wild yeast spores and *Lacto bacilli sp.* occur naturally in the air and can be "captured" quite easily. Mix a couple cups of good bread flour with two cups warm water (bottled, well, or distilled) in a bowl (glass, ceramic, or plastic) and stir well. I like to use a whisk to introduce additional air into the mixture. Cover the bowl with cheese cloth and set it outdoors for a couple of days. Stir the mixture a couple of times everyday. In 2-3 days you should see bubbles forming in the flour and water mixture. This indicates you've indeed captured wild yeast spores and they're feeding on the nutrients in the flour. Feed the mixture with another cup each of flour and water. Stir and let sit for another day or two. When more bubbles form, you can test for an active culture by taking a teaspoon of the starter and stirring in a pinch of baking soda. If it foams up you have an active starter. This test is nothing more than basic high school chemistry. Lactic acid reacts with the base in the soda and the foam results. Note: Since yeast spores are temperature sensitive and will grow faster in a warm environment, you'll have greater success if you do this in the warmer months. Also you can do this indoors, but air filtration systems in most modern homes make it much more difficult, if not impossible, because the natural bacteria in the air is removed.

The second method I've used is basically the same except I add a pinch of salt, a tablespoon of vinegar, and two tablespoons of sugar or honey to the initial mixture. The sugar provides additional nutrients for the yeast spores to "eat".

Sourdough Do's and Don'ts

Do not use self-rising flour. Self-rising flour contains chemical leavening agents such as baking powder and baking soda which will kill the yeast spores.

Do use well, bottled, or distilled water when feeding a starter or trying to start your own starter. Use of chlorinated water may interfere with the wild yeast spores metabolic processes.

Do store your starter in a glass, plastic, or ceramic container. Sourdough starters are acidic. If stored in a metal container, or even a glass jar with a metal lid, there is a risk of corrosion which will taint or kill the starter.

Do use a glass, plastic, or ceramic bowl during the first proof. If a metal bowl is used, the acids present in the starter can cause the same problems as with storage. It's OK to use stainless steel bowls for the actual mixing of the bread and the second proof.

Do store your starter in the fridge. Some folks have told me they have frozen their starters, but I've had great difficulty in re-activating frozen starters. (It's well documented that old time cooks often slept with their starters to keep them warm and from freezing during the winter months.)

Do use your starter as frequently as possible. Sourdough starters are like many other things, the more they are used, the better they become. The yeast spores and bacteria in starters used on a regular basis react more quickly and more robustly which enhances their leavening effect on the breads.

Do not discard a starter that has been stored for a long time which has caused the hooch to turn dark. Allow the starter to come to room temperature, stir the hooch back into the semi-solids that settled to the bottom of the storage container. Feed the starter about every twelve hours with a 1:1 ratio of flour to water for 2-3 days. The yeast spores and bacteria do not die during extended storage periods, but rather they go into a dormant state. It will take several feedings to rejuvenate a starter that has been stored for a long time, but it can be done. (Many a starter has been "tossed" when an over zealous, but uninformed, person cleaned the refrigerator.)

Do keep at least two separate containers of your starter. I do this with my starters so that I can take one to camp with me and leave the other one home. I call the one at home my "insurance dough".

DO THIS EVERYTIME YOU FEED YOUR STARTER. EVERYTIME YOU FEED YOUR STARTER, RETURN SOME OF THE SPONGE TO YOUR STARTER STORAGE CONTAINER, BEFORE ADDING ANY ADDITIONAL INGREDIENTS TO THE SPONGE.

DO BE PATIENT WHEN MAKING SOURDOUGH BREAD. Sourdough starters leaven bread much more slowly than their domestic counter parts. Allow plenty of time for both "proofs"!

Do not give up if your first attempt(s) are not very successful! Every accomplished sourdough cook will tell you the same thing if asked. There is no exact formula or equation that will yield perfect sourdough bread on your first attempt! These same folks, including this author, will also tell you that you'll develop a "feel" for sourdough much like a brick layer can "feel" the state of his mortar when laying bricks. By knowing the "feel" when he scoops some up with his trowel, the experienced brick layer knows if the mortar is correctly mixed. It is that "feel" that separates the novice from the expert.

47

Getting Started

Getting your first sourdough starter is like getting your first horse. There is an initial period when you need to get acquainted. Like pack horses in a pack string, each starter has it's own quirks, individual characteristics, and pace at which they work best. Once you gain experience in taking care of and using your starter, your enjoyment and success will increase.

I recommend that beginners get proficient at making sourdough pancakes before stepping up to baking breads. One merely has to feed the starter to make a sponge, return a portion of their sponge back into it's storage container, and add four ingredients to have delicious sourdough pancakes. (We've reprinted our favorite sourdough pancake recipe below that is from our first cookbook.) Once experienced in feeding your starter and having a "feel" for the sponge, it's much easier to tackle the nuances and vagaries of using wild yeast to make and bake sourdough bread.

The Purists vs. The Impatient

In our fast-paced society some folks, like the author, will sometimes take a short cut in making sourdough bread which causes great weeping, wailing, and gnashing of teeth among those who consider themselves "purists of the highest order". Since proofing with sourdough takes so long, some folks hasten the leavening process by adding domestic yeast to the sponge. (Do not add domestic yeast to your starter, only to the sponge!) Though sacrilege to the purists, I don't consider this a "sin", per se, but a personal choice. Of course there are pro's and con's to taking this shortcut. Since lactic acid produced by *Lacto bacilli sp.* provides the characteristic "sour" taste, using "booster cables", i.e., domestic yeast, the shortened leavening period does not allow the bacteria to produce as much lactic acid which results in a less sour taste. However, if the starter you're using has been recently fed, there will be enough remaining lactic acid to get the flavor you want.

Most commercial bakeries who market sourdough bread use this same shortcut. The next time you're in the bread section of your local grocery store, check the ingredients list on all the sourdough bread on the shelf. Along with "sourdough culture", you will on almost all occasions see "yeast" as well. In other words, the commercial bakeries do not have the time to allow their sourdough culture to naturally leaven the bread so they use "booster cables" to speed things up just like you may wish to do as well.

Once you graduate to making and baking basic sourdough bread, you're ready to take the next step. Once confidence has been made in making bread, I encourage beginning to experiment with sourdough. For example, adding a tablespoon each of fresh chopped basil, rosemary, and/or oregano to the sponge changes basic sourdough bread into awesome Italian Herb Bread! Or, one can add a little additional sugar or honey to the sponge and make sweet dough for cinnamon rolls. Once you have the "feel" for sourdough, only your imagination limits your sourdough creations.

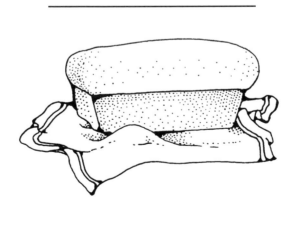

Sourdough Hotcake Batter

Ingredients:

2 cups starter
1 Tbsp. sugar
1 tsp. salt
1 egg
1 tsp. baking soda (slightly more suits me)

Mix together well the starter, sugar, salt, and egg by hand. Mix baking soda in a dab of water to prevent lumps. Stir baking soda mixture into batter stirring only as much as necessary to mix. Batter should rise to about double, looks kind of like meringue. If you want berries, or other goodies, add to batter. Spoon onto hot griddle, turn when bubbles pop, test for done by pressing corner of spatula into center of hotcake. If it springs back, it is done.

Cee Dub's sourdough rolls hot out of the Dutch oven. YUM! YUM!   Vernon Hayes Photo

Sourdough Rolls

Ingredients:

1 cup starter
½ cup milk at room temperature (buttermilk
        makes even better sourdough bread)
1 tsp. yeast dissolved
4 Tbsp. water
1 Tbsp. olive oil
1 Tbsp. sugar
Pinch of salt
1-2 cups all purpose unbleached flour

NOTE: This recipe makes one average size loaf or a family size batch of rolls. To make larger quantities, increase all ingredients proportionately.

Dissolve the yeast in the water and half the sugar and let sit for a few minutes. This will jump start the yeast. Stir in all the remaining ingredients except for the flour. Gradually stir in remaining flour until the dough forms a ball and pulls away from the sides of the bowl. Turn the dough onto a floured cutting board or pastry cloth and knead for about ten minutes until dough has a satin like surface. Place kneaded dough in a lightly oiled bowl and cover with a clean dish towel. Let sit in a warm location to proof. When it's doubled in size, punch it down and knead for about a minute before pinching off ping pong sized balls and rolling them between your palms for rolls. Place in a 12" DO with about ½" between rolls. Set in a warm place and allow to raise until the rolls touch. Bake for 20-25 minutes with 5-8 briquets on the bottom and 18-22 on the top.

Words of Wisdom

When a recipe calls for crumbled bacon, dice it before frying for more even cooking.

SINGLE MALT
CHERRY PECAN ROLLS

These rolls are a Las Piedras Ranch tradition and made only when Randy Riney makes a trip to the ranch. They came about when one good tradition over time gave rise to another. Both Randy and I have aged a few years since I first came to Las Piedras to cook. Until moving to Texas, Randy and I saw each other only once a year when I came down to cook for the Cattle Barons Hunt. At that first meeting we found that among many other things, that we both enjoyed sips of single malt Scotch, poured one "skosh" at a time. And…therein lies the basis for the tradition.

Just like a puppy, Randy wanted to run with the old dogs. So when I showed up the second and subsequent years for the hunt, Randy made sure he showed up with a good bottle of single malt. After supper he'd pour us each a "skosh" and we'd commence to catch up after not seeing each other for a year; and, solve all the world's problems along the way. By the grey light of dawn, we'd have things pretty-well solved and under control, so we thought; and, with just a "skosh" left in the Scotch bottle.

As we age our requirement for sleep often increases and one night I found myself having a hard time keeping ahead of the puppy! As I recall it was about 3:00 am when I realized that if I didn't do something to keep busy, I'd fall asleep and Randy would then have bragging rights. It was a case of start moving or perish! So I decided to make some sweet rolls with what I had on hand. Below is what turned out, and is now expected!

—— Single Malt Cherry Pecan Rolls ——

Ingredients:

2 cups milk at room temperature
½ cup of sugar or honey

3 Tbsp. vegetable oil
2 pkg. yeast dissolved in ½ cup water- add 1 Tbsp.
        of sugar or honey
½ tsp. salt
4-5 cups of flour

Topping:

1 8 oz. jar of maraschino cherries,
        drained and chopped
1 cup chopped pecans
1 cup packed brown sugar
1 stick of butter, melted
Cinnamon, to taste
Nutmeg, to taste

Combine the first three ingredients in a large mixing bowl and stir well. When the dissolved yeast begins to froth add it to this mixture along with the salt. Gradually stir in additional flour until too stiff to stir. Turn out onto a well floured cutting board and knead for about 10 minutes. Wash your mixing bowl and lightly oil it. When through kneading, place the dough in the bowl and cover it with a dish towel. Let dough rise until double in size. When doubled in size, punch the dough down and knead for another couple of minutes. On a large well-floured cutting board, roll the dough out into a rectangular shape. The dough should be about ¼" thick. Spread the melted butter over the entire surface of the dough with a pastry brush; and, then sprinkle it with the brown sugar. Sprinkle the cherry pieces and pecan bits evenly over the dough. Sprinkle the cinnamon and nutmeg over the dough, to taste. Carefully roll the dough up into a long cylinder. Cut the rolls about an inch thick with dental floss and place in a 14" DO with about a half inch between rolls. Let rise until the rolls are all touching and then bake for 30 to 40 minutes with 8-10 briquets underneath and 29-32 on top. In a home oven, bake at 365 degrees for 25 to 30 minutes, or until golden brown. Frost, if desired. Serve with plenty of hot coffee!

HEALTHY COOKIN'
DUTCH OVEN STYLE

I published my first cookbook over a decade ago. I vividly remember the first putdown of that book and Dutch oven cooking. It occurred at a public appearance to promote my book. A lady came up to the table where I was signing cookbooks and picked up my display copy. She leafed through it for a few seconds and then set it down as she made this comment, "I don't like Dutch oven cooking because all it amounts to are gut bombs full of fat and cheese!" She prejudged the cookbook before getting to the short section on cooking light that I'd included. Dutch ovens shouldn't get the bad rap...because it's the recipe ingredients that determine whether a recipe is "light" or if it is a gut bomb."

Before Pen and I started this project we surfed the web looking for nutritional analysis software. We wanted to include nutritional information for recipes in this cookbook. We shelved that idea when it became obvious that to do so would require cutting the number of recipes, tips, stories, and photos.

So, we urge you to check out nutritional analysis software available on the web. Just "google" words such as "nuitritional analysis" or "recipe calculator" or "nutritional calculator". Our personal choice is available at www.dvo.com . The capability of the DVO software far exceeds the computer literacy of this author. Suffice it to say it works great. In addition DVO has a great selection of cookbooks and recipes available as downloads or on CD's, including my first two cookbooks: Cee Dub's Dutch Oven & Other Camp Cookin' and More Cee Dub's Dutch Oven & Other Camp Cookin'.

Mexican Cornbread

Ingredients:

1 Tbsp. oil
1 lb. hamburger
1 large onion, chopped
1 cup yellow or white cornmeal
2 eggs
1 cup milk or half and half
½ tsp. baking soda
¾ tsp. cumin
½ tsp. salt
1 15 oz. can cream-style corn
½ lb. grated Pepper Jack cheese
4 jalapeno peppers, seeded and chopped

Heat oil in a large skillet. Brown meat and onion in skillet until done. Drain and set aside. In a bowl beat eggs. Add cornmeal, milk or half and half, soda, cumin, and salt. Add corn to batter. Grease a large cast iron skillet or 12" Dutch oven. Preheat the skillet or DO, using 6-8 briquets underneath. Pour one-half the batter into the skillet or DO. Sprinkle the cheese on evenly. Layer the meat and onions on the cheese. Sprinkle on the peppers. Pour the remaining batter on top. In the oven bake at 350 degrees for 45 to 50 minutes; or, cover the DO and bake for 45 to 50 minutes using 6-8 briquets under the DO and 18-22 briquets on the lid.

Pecan Date Loaf

Ingredients:

2 eggs
1 cup brown sugar, packed
1 Tbsp. butter, melted
¾ cup flour
½ tsp. baking powder
¼ tsp. salt
1 cup chopped pecans
1 cup chopped dates

Beat eggs well. Add sugar and butter; beat. Mix flour, baking powder, and salt; add to eggs and sugar mixture. Mix in pecans and dates. Place in greased and floured loaf pan. Bake at 350 degrees until light brown, about an hour.

Monkey Bread

Ingredients:

3 cans biscuits, cut into quarters
¾ cup white sugar
1 tsp. cinnamon
1 cup chopped pecans, optional
1 stick butter
¾ cup brown sugar

Spray a 12" Dutch oven with non-stick cooking spray. Pour nuts evenly in the bottom of DO, if desired. In a small bowl, mix white sugar and cinnamon together. Roll each biscuit piece in mixture and place in DO. Melt butter and add brown sugar. Pour over sugared biscuit pieces. Cover DO and bake at 350 degrees for 30 to 40 minutes using 6-8 briquets under the oven and 18-22 briquets on the lid. Remove from DO and serve. Serves 10 to 12.

New Mexico
Blue Cornbread

Ingredients:

½ cup butter or margarine, melted
1 cup blue cornmeal
1/3 cup whole wheat pastry flour, or
       whole wheat pancake mix
2/3 cup unbleached flour
2 tsp. baking powder
½ tsp. baking soda
1 tsp. salt
1 large egg
1 1/3 cups buttermilk

Lightly grease a 12" Dutch oven. Preheat DO for 15-20 minutes using 20-22 briquets on the lid and 9 underneath. Mix ingredients quickly in order given, beating only until mixed well. Pour batter into preheated DO and bake at high heat, 425 degrees, for about 20-25 minutes until light brown on top.

Sherry and Delmar Hiller
Carolyn and Danny Wheat
Hunt, Texas

S Hiller, S Truitt, D Hiller, and K & J Rainey - DO Clinic
Fall 2006   Truitt Photo

57

Cranberry Muffins

Ingredients:

5 oz. fresh, frozen, or dried cranberries
2 ¼ cups all-purpose flour
1 ½ tsp. baking powder
½ tsp. baking soda
½ tsp. salt
3 Tbsp. oil
3 Tbsp. butter
¾ cup sugar
2 large eggs, slightly beaten
2/3 cup orange juice
¾ cup coarsely chopped walnuts

Preheat oven to 375 degrees. Line muffin cups with cupcake liners. Coarsely chop the cranberries and set aside. In a medium bowl, mix together the flour, baking powder, baking soda, and salt; set aside. In a small saucepan, combine the oil and butter and heat until the butter melts. Remove from heat and stir in the sugar; but it will not dissolve. Set aside. In a large bowl, stir together the eggs and orange juice. Stir in the butter and sugar mixture. Add dry ingredients and mix until moistened. Add cranberries and walnuts. Fill muffin cups until nearly full of batter. Bake for 18 to 20 minutes, until golden brown and the tops are springy to the touch. Cool on a wire rack. Makes 12 to 14 muffins.

Betty Welch
Pocatello, Idaho

Breakfast

TIME & TEMPERATURE

Most folks new to Dutch oven cookin' often express apprehension or are intimidated by the thought of trying to prepare a meal with nothing more than a couple of clumsy black pots and some charcoal briquets. But, whether teaching a clinic or giving a public demonstration, I try to allay their fears by repeating one phrase over and over. I tell them, "Cooking is nothing more than managing time and temperature!"

Especially for the beginner it's important to start with simple recipes and better yet a recipe the person is already familiar with. With few exceptions, recipes from one's home kitchen can be adapted easily for use in a Dutch oven. The reality of the situation is that a Dutch oven is just another type of cooking vessel; but, the more important issue is that of the heat source used for cooking the food. "Keep It Simple S+%#*& (KISS)" is a good motto for new Dutch oven cooks.

I don't mean to trivialize cooking in a kitchen, but there are a host of issues the indoor cook does not have to deal with. For example, the outside temperature, wind, and precipitation don't affect the results for someone cooking in a home kitchen. Besides not having to worry about the weather, the indoor cook merely has to twist a dial to achieve the desired heat for any given recipe rather than start a bunch of charcoal briquets that will last only so long. Short of a power outage or the timer turning off the oven, the indoor cook can set the heat for an indefinite time, especially if slow roasting a large roast, turkey, etc.

Time after time as I do public demonstrations I'm asked, "What is the secret to managing the heat on a Dutch oven?" Not to disappoint anyone, but part of the answer is that way more common sense is involved than magic. Rather than twist a dial to obtain the desired temperature, the Dutch oven cook must add or subtract briquets or wood coals to achieve the proper temperature knowing he or she will only have that heat for a finite period of time.

Some Dutch oven cookbook authors give very specific directions as to exactly how many briquets should be used to obtain a certain temperature or cook a specific recipe. But, what these authors do not delve into is that their directions are for what I call static conditions, i.e., moderate temperatures of from 50-80 degrees and no wind. Trust me, their formulas, ratios, and equations don't work very well if you're out there trying to cook for a bunch of hungry folks, like hunters, and the temperature has dropped into the thirties or forties with a 20 mph wind blowing.

In my cookbooks I've tried to broaden the window and not get too specific. For example, I say as a standard to put 6-8 briquets underneath the 12" Dutch and 18-22 on top for baking biscuits. Another broad stroke to differentiate conditions, if baking biscuits on a hot July afternoon, you can get away with using 6 briquets on the bottom and 18 on the top. The biscuits will bake to a perfect golden brown in about 25 to 30 minutes. On the other hand, if it's in the forties and a stiff breeze blowing and I use that same heat scheme my biscuits will take a lot longer and probably won't brown up as well. So to bake biscuits in colder conditions, I do what you do when cooking in the kitchen when more heat is needed; I turn up the heat, that is, use more briquets.

Keep in mind that especially when baking, the amount of heat on the bottom is more critical. More specifically relating to briquet placement, for baking biscuits in a 12" Dutch oven in the warm weather scenario, I will place five of my briquets evenly spaced in a circle slightly less than the diameter of my oven with one in the center of the circle. Basic common sense tells us that if it's colder we're going to need more heat to get the biscuits done in the same amount of time. To accomplish this I simply add more heat. On the bottom I squeeze a couple more briquets into the circle and place two in the center of the circle. Note, keep your bottom briquets evenly spaced and do not allow any of them to touch each other. If you have bottom briquets touching, you will end up with a hot spot and will likely over brown the bottoms. On the top of the oven I place the briquets around the outside flange of the lid and place about three in the middle. In colder conditions, crowd the briquets closer together, squeezing in 2 to 4 more briquets.

To reiterate what I said earlier, once you have your grub in the Dutch oven, the only thing you should have to worry about is "Time and Temperature". Yet, there are always those who feel better if given specific directions on heat management.

Words of Wisdom

Whenever possible, use flexible cutting boards in the preparation of raw meats, especially poultry After you finish the prep work, clean and sanitize them to prevent possible cross contamination.

Breakfast Chorizo Quesadillas

Ingredients:

1 pkg. chorizo sausage
1 pkg. flour tortillas
1 cup grated cheese of your choice

Crumble the chorizo sausage into skillet and brown thoroughly. Set aside to stay warm. Butter tortillas on one side. In a separate skillet, preferrably cast iron, lay buttered side down in hot skillet, sprinkle cooked chorizo and some cheese in each one. Add another tortilla, buttered side up. When the bottom tortilla gets toasty, flip the quesadilla over and cook the other side. Repeat the process for as many as needed for campers. Cut like pizza slices. Serve with pineapple chunks or slices.

Sherry and Delmar Hiller
Carolyn and Danny Wheat
Hunt, Texas

—— Brian's Breakfast Tacos ——

Ingredients:

1 lb. bacon
6-10 eggs
Milk, if desired
1 tsp. chili powder
1 tsp. garlic powder
1 cup fresh salsa
1 cup chopped fresh cilantro
8 corn or flour tortillas
Sour cream, as garnishment

In a medium pan, fry bacon, set bacon to the side, and save roughly one-fourth the grease. Break the bacon strips into bite size pieces. Mix eggs in a bowl; add milk, if desired. Begin scrambling in frying pan with bacon grease. Add chili powder and garlic powder. When eggs are starting to become firm, add the salsa and mix well. Just before the eggs are done, add bacon back to pan. Add cilantro and mix well. Serve over warm tortillas with sour cream.

Brian Welch
Boise, Idaho

—— Cinnamon Honey Butter ——

Ingredients:

1 cup butter, slightly softened
1 tsp. ground cinnamon
½ cup honey

Combine all ingredients in a small mixing bowl and beat until smooth. Serve on muffins, toast, bagels, French toast, or pancakes. Refrigerate leftovers. Makes 1 1/3 cups.

Fant's Lake D'Arbonne
———— Breakfast Casserole ————

The 2007 National DOG (Dutch Oven Gathering) was held at Lake D'Arbonne State Park in Louisiana. What a beautiful slice of heaven! Needless to say, lots of good food and good times were enjoyed by all who attended. As part of the events, several cookoffs were held, one being "Breakfast" entrees. Fant told us that he had decided to enter the "Breakfast" competition because he really liked the prize offered for first place. So while driving to Lake D'Arbonne, he created the following recipe in his mind's eye. And, oh yes, by the way, Fant won First Place!

Ingredients:

6 potatoes, shredded ¼ inch width
Salt and pepper, to taste
1 Tbsp. butter
1 lb. hot breakfast sausage
1 lb. bacon
1 medium onion, minced
1 can Rotel™ diced tomatoes with chilies; or,
 1 can Mexican diced tomatoes, drained
18 eggs
8 oz. sharp cheddar cheese, grated

Preheat a 12" Dutch oven. Combine the shredded potatoes with 1 beaten egg to bind the potatoes. Season with salt and pepper. Spray the DO with non-stick spray and then coat with butter. Press the potato mixture into the DO to form a crust that extends about two inches up the side. The crust should be about a quarter inch thick. Bake the potato crust using about 9 briquets under the DO, rim the lid using about 18 briquets, and place about 4 in the middle. While the crust is baking, brown the sausage and bacon in another DO or cast iron frying pan. Add the onions and the drained tomatoes and cook

Fant's First Place prize for his Breakfast
Casserole at the Nat'l DOG in Louisiana
Fant Steele Photo Collection

thoroughly. Drain off any excess liquid or grease. Break
and thoroughly whisk the 17 eggs in a bowl. Add the
eggs to the meat mixture and scramble the eggs. When
the crust is done, about an hour, remove it from the heat.
Press the cooked egg and meat mixture into the crust.
Put the cheese on top. Place the top heat back on the
DO and let it cook about another 15 minutes until cheese
melts. Remove from heat, let it rest for about 5 minutes,
then serve. NOTE: Soaking potatoes in salted water before
cooking will keep the potatoes from turning brown.

Fant Steele
Rochester, Minnesota

Camp Quiche **

Ingredients:

1 Tbsp. butter
½ cup chopped onion
¾ cup diced cooked ham
1 medium tomato, chopped
2 cups biscuit/baking mix
½ cup water
1 cup shredded Swiss or cheddar cheese
2 eggs
¼ cup milk
¼ tsp. dill weed
¼ tsp. salt
¼ tsp. pepper
2 green onions, thinly sliced

In a skillet, heat butter and sauté onion in butter until tender. Stir in ham and tomato and set aside. In a bowl, combine biscuit mix and water, mixing well. Grease or spray a 13 x 9 inch baking dish or 12" Dutch oven. Press dough mixture onto the bottom and up the sides one inch. If dough is somewhat wet and sticky, dip fingers in flour or baking mix to enable working dough more easily. Spread ham mixture over crust and sprinkle with cheese. In a bowl, beat the eggs, milk, dill, salt, and pepper. Pour mixture over cheese. Sprinkle green onions on top. Bake uncovered in the oven at 350 degrees. If using DO, cover and bake using 6-8 briquets under oven and 18-22 briquets on the lid. Bake for 25 to 30 minutes or until knife inserted in center comes out clean. Serve with a dollop of sour cream and fruit. Serves 6 to 8.

** A photo of this recipe is featured at the beginning of the "Breakfast" section.

SICK CHICKENS

It is a fact of life that if you are a parent, own a dog, a cat, or a horse, it's not a matter of IF you'll be embarrassed by them, but a matter of WHEN! Try bragging about how well-trained your bird dog is, and as sure as I'm sitting here, on your next bird hunting trip, he'll forget every command he's been taught and act like he just escaped from a canine funny farm. Tell someone, "old Black Jack horse here is the gentlest, most even-tempered horse I've ever owned." Then as soon as your friend mounts up, old Black Jack throws a white-eyed, snot-blowin' fit and puts the guy who you hope is still your friend in the hospital. Since kids can talk, as well as act, compounds the likelihood they'll embarrass you. Anyway… you get the picture!

My Dad started dragging me along on hunting trips with him and his buddies when my age was still in the single digits. I lived for the weekends in October and November because I knew we were either going to go pheasant hunting or deer hunting. We usually took my Uncle Vern's old Pontiac station wagon. I wish I had a picture of that old "Woody" but I don't. As the only kid on these trips I got to sit in the middle of the front seat 'cause my legs were the shortest. Dad and his buds thought their hunting trip discussions were over my head. Well, literally they were 'cause I was the shortest, but figuratively they were wrong. Those hunting trips jump started that portion of my education that occurred outside the classroom. (That's another whole book.)

Saturday morning would find Dad and me up extra early to get the chores done before Uncle Vern showed up with the rest of the guys. One of my chores was making sure the chickens had feed and water. Then we'd throw our stuff in the back of the old "Woody" before heading out. Those drives through the dark early morning hours contributed significantly to my education. But, I'm getting off track again.

Near where we planned to hunt we'd pull into a roadside café and get breakfast. On the day in question I ordered my usual, sausage and eggs. Things went to hell when the waitress put my breakfast in front of me. There was something WRONG with the eggs. The yolks were pale, and I mean PALE, YELLOW! Our free ranging chickens that I'd fed just a couple of hours earlier layed eggs with yolks with a deep orange color, more ORANGE than an orange itself. I nudged my Dad and said that there was something wrong with my eggs. First he asked what was wrong, and when I told him he just told me to be quiet and eat. No way! Of course kids were supposed to be seen and not heard, so when I said in a voice too loud, "Daaad, these eggs came from SICK chickens!", Dad threatened me with never going on another hunting trip if I didn't SHUT UP AND EAT!.

Under EXTREME duress, I choked those eggs down; but the story didn't end there. I almost caused a wreck when I jumped across Dad's lap and rolled the window down before hurling that order of sausage and eggs down the side of Uncle Vern's Pontiac after we left the café. Though Dad relented on his threat to never take me hunting, it was years before he would let me order anything except pancakes or waffles when we stopped for breakfast on hunting trips.

These years later I will still choose eggs from organically raised free-ranging chickens over the store-bought variety. And to this very day, when I make egg noodles using just the yolks and have egg whites left over, Pen has the pleasure of eating the scrambled whites, and does so out of my view. To me, the color of scrambled whites brings back thoughts of "sick chickens" having laid those eggs and my stomach does a little flip.

Ice Cream Pancakes

Use your favorite flavor of ice cream, melted, in place of milk or water added to the pancake mix to make the batter. And, instead of using syrup for these cakes, just sprinkle on some powdered sugar. Be creative with the flavors! NOTE: Because of the additional sugar in the ice cream, pay close attention while the cakes are on the griddle to keep from scorching.

Hobart Manns
Portland, Oregon

Tex-Mex Frittata

Ingredients:

2 Tbsp. butter
1 small onion, chopped
1 cup corn niblets, drained
2 Tbsp. jalapenos or
    diced green chilies
8 eggs
½ cup milk
½ tsp. cumin
Salt and pepper, to taste
¾ cup grated cheddar or Pepper Jack cheese

Heat butter in a 10" Dutch oven. Add onion and cook until soft. Add the corn and jalapenos or chilies. Cook for another minute. In a bowl, whisk together eggs, milk, cumin, salt and pepper. Cover the onion, corn, and jalapenos or chilies mixture with cheese. Gently pour egg mixture over cheese. Cover and bake at 375 degrees for about 30 minutes using 5 briquets underneath and 12-14 briquets on the lid. Serve with salsa and sour cream. Serves 6 to 8.

Pen's Southwest
—————— Breakfast Casserole ——————

Ingredients:

1 lb. breakfast sausage
1 ½ tsp. cumin
4 cloves garlic, minced
1 dozen eggs, lightly beaten
3 cups milk *
* For a decadent variation, use half and half,
    whipping cream, or a combination
2 tsp. dry mustard
1 tsp. salt
2 Tbsp. melted butter
6 cups cubed bread
2 cups shredded sharp cheddar cheese
1 tsp. pepper
¾ cup sliced mushrooms
½ cup chopped green pepper
½ cup thinly sliced green onions
1 medium tomato, chopped
4 Tbsp. chopped cilantro, optional
8 Tbsp. salsa

In a large skillet, cook sausage over medium-high heat,
stirring frequently just until no longer pink. Mix in cumin
and garlic while cooking. In large mixing bowl, combine
eggs, milk, mustard, and salt; stir well. Put melted butter
in a 12" Dutch oven. Distribute half of the cubed bread
on the butter. Sprinkle with half the cheese, and half
the pepper. Top with half the sausage mixture. Add
half the mushrooms, green pepper, green onions, and
tomato. Drizzle half the salsa over the ingredients. Repeat
layering using remaining bread, cheese, pepper, sausage,
vegetables, and salsa. Pour egg mixture over casserole
ingredients. Bake covered about 60 minutes or until eggs
are set, using 6-8 briquets under the Dutch and 18-20

briquets on the lid. If baking in the oven, bake uncovered at 325 degrees for 60 minutes or until eggs are set. Tent with foil or cover with Dutch oven lid if top browns too quickly.

Penny Welch
Mountain Home, Texas

Words of Wisdom

 To help eliminate weevils in flour or corn meal, first freeze the items in their original packaging before putting them in canisters.

Dad's Hotcakes

Ingredients:

¼ cup sugar
¼ cup shortening, or oil
2 eggs
2 cups buttermilk
1¼ tsp. baking soda
¾ tsp. baking powder
1 tsp. salt
2 cups flour
1 tsp. lemon extract

Cream together sugar and shortening. Add eggs and buttermilk and mix all together. Then mix in baking soda, baking powder, and salt. Next, add and mix in flour, making the batter the consistency of cake batter. If it is too thick, add more buttermilk. Mix in the lemon extract. (This was Dad's magic ingredient that made his hotcakes different from all others.) Spoon the batter onto a hot griddle. Flip each pancake when the surface is covered with tiny bubbles. Cook until the bottom is golden brown.

Carol Hampton
Bonners Ferry, Idaho

— Scrambled Eggs and Tomatoes —

Ingredients:

1 Roma tomato, diced
1 tsp. chopped basil, or
¼ tsp. dried basil
2 eggs
2 tsp. water
1 clove garlic, minced
Seasonings to taste
½ cup grated cheddar cheese, optional

Combine tomato and basil in a small bowl and set aside. In another bowl, beat the egg, water, garlic, and seasonings. In a small cast iron skillet coated with nonstick cooking spray, cook and stir egg mixture over medium heat until egg is nearly set. Add the tomato mixture and cook until eggs are set. Melt cheese on top. Serve with a bagel, an English muffin, or toast. Serves 2.

— Sandy's Breakfast Casserole —

Ingredients:

1 lb. sausage, browned
6-8 slices bread, trimmed and buttered on both sides
1 lb. cheddar cheese, grated
6-8 eggs, beaten
2 cups milk or half and half
1 4 oz. can chopped green chiles, optional

Arrange buttered bread slices flat in 9" x 12" casserole dish or 12" Dutch oven. Put cooked sausage on top of bread. Put one-half cheese on sausage. Mix eggs, milk, and chiles, and pour over bread, meat, and cheese. Sprinkle remaining cheese on top. Bake covered for 45 to 60 minutes at 350 degrees. If using Dutch oven, use 6-8 briquets underneath and 18-22 briquets on the lid.

Sandy Riney
Montgomery, Texas

══ FLOWERS IN HUNTIN' CAMP ? ══

In my twenty-one years as a game warden, I visited more huntin' camps than I can count. Also,after adding in all the huntin' camps I've shared with my Dad, my wife and our sons, plus friends over the last 45 years, it's my guess that the total runs into the thousands. Probably the closest thing to flowers in any of those camps might have been the occasional floral print table cloth that after wear and tear at home ended up in the camp kitchen. But, that all changed a few days before Valentine's Day in 2000.

This trip from Idaho to San Antonio, Texas resulted from a chance meeting with Dwain Riney of Las Piedras Ranch the fall before at an antique show in Round Top, Texas. Dwain really piqued my curiosity with his stories of hunting free ranging exotics such as Aoudad, Corsican Rams, Axis, Sika, and Fallow Deer, along with feral hogs, at Las Piedras. That thirty minute conversation ended up with Dwain and his wife, Sandy, inviting me to Las Piedras to cook for a hunt they donate each year to The Montgomery County Cattle Barons Ball where the hunt is auctioned off to benefit the American Cancer Society. Our deal was that I would be traveling at my own expense and would donate my services as their "celebrity camp cook". In return Dwain assured me there would be enough time away from my Dutch ovens to do a little hunting. That was all the encouragement I needed to accept their invitation to a huntin' camp in Texas.

I'd flown from Idaho into San Antonio, Texas, to meet Dwain, not really knowing exactly what to expect. Other than a few phone calls during the previous intervening months, Dwain and I were pretty close to strangers as we headed for Kerrville from the San Antonio airport. Dwain, ever the consummate host, not only told me more about the ranch, but also pointed out places of interest as we headed down I-10. Before heading out to the ranch we needed to stop in Kerrville to buy groceries. Grub for eight guys for a week of hunting required three full shopping carts and almost two hours. By the time we finished at the store, at least from my perspective, I felt I was getting to know Dwain fairly well. We were hurrying as best we could so that Dwain could show me more of the country on our way into the ranch. He hoped to make it in while it was still daylight. I thought that a quick stop at a sporting goods store to buy my non-resident hunting license was our last stop. Wrong!

Just before we cleared town, Dwain said "Damn", hit the brakes, made a U-turn, and headed back into town. Trust me, I became more than a bit confused when Dwain stopped at a florist's shop and said, "I'll be right back!" Now up to this point, I'm thinking we're doing the usual stuff before heading to huntin' camp for a week! But, when Dwain came back out to the truck with two huge containers of cut flowers, I start thinking to myself that something hinky is about to happen!

Dwain didn't volunteer anything about the flowers, and I was smart enough to keep my mouth shut as we headed west on Highway 41 to the ranch. Things just were not adding up in my mind, such as: it's the week before Valentine's Day, we're headed to huntin' camp where I've been told I would be cooking for eight GUYS, we are driving west into the setting sun, and Dwain's wife Sandy is home, which is about a five hour drive east of the ranch!

As the miles went by, my suspicions grew greater. The scenario that kept running through my mind went something like this. Before getting to Las Piedras we would pull into an isolated ranch, where Dwain would take the flowers in and leave me in the truck. I could almost hear him say, "We don't need to talk about this stop…to anyone!" In looking back now, I jumped to this conclusion because of several situations during my career as a game warden where I encountered guys who used huntin' camp as an opportunity to spend some cozy times in the woods with someone other than their wives!

The sun had just gone down when we left the pavement and turned south off of Highway 41 onto the

Hackberry Road. Dwain showed me lots of critters as we drove down the road through stands of oak, juniper, and the occasional mesquite tree. It was the first time I'd ever seen free ranging exotics and it took my mind off the backseat full of flowers. By the time we pulled into the ranch house it was completely dark. After opening up the house, we built a fire in the fire pit to grill steaks and started to unload the truck. As we carried the two floral arrangements into the house, Dwain finally put my mind at ease when he said, "Sandy would have a fit if I ever brought guests out here and didn't have fresh flowers!" The mystery of the flowers in huntin' camp was solved!

It was two or three years before I got up enough nerve to tell this story to Sandy, and to this day every time I relate this story, her infectious laughter and the twinkle in her eyes tells me all my worries were unfounded!

Author's Post Script: Little did I realize that eight years later Pen and I would call Las Piedras Ranch home for the first two years after our move from Idaho to Texas, and this cookbook would be written in the ranch house huntin' camp I carried those flowers into that February night in 2000. Since that year we've helped the Riney family with entertaining many groups of hunters. And, we never forget to include fresh cut flowers on our shopping lists!

Butterfly in the Welch flower garden at LPR summer 2008
Welch Photo Collection

Salads

—— Avocado and Citrus Salad ——

Ingredient:

2 medium grapefruit
3 oranges
6 cups salad greens
1 ripe avocado, peeled and sliced
¼ cup slivered almonds
½ cup oil
1/3 cup sugar
3 Tbsp. vinegar
1 tsp. finely chopped onion
½ tsp. dry mustard
2 tsp. poppy seeds
½ tsp. salt

Peel grapefruit and oranges. Slice into bite-size pieces and place in bowl. Add greens, avocado, and almonds. Combine other ingredients in a jar with a tight-fitting lid, and shake well. Pour over salad and toss. Serves 6.

—— Celery Seed Dressing ——

Ingredients:

½ cup sugar
1 tsp. mustard
1 tsp. salt
2 tsp. celery seed
2 Tbsp. grated onion
1/3 cup vinegar
2 tsp. creamed horseradish
1 cup salad oil

In a blender combine and mix all ingredients except oil and one-half of the vinegar. Pour oil in slowly and add remaining vinegar slowly. Blend well and chill.

Nancy Boylan
Longview, Washington

Words of Wisdom

To keep wooden utensils and cutting boards looking new, occasionally rub them down with mineral oil.

To restore a snow white color to your plastic cutting boards, take them to the car wash and use the high pressure wash. This also works well for coolers and plastic camp boxes. A 2,500 psi home power washer works even better.

Cauliflower Broccoli Toss

Ingredients:

2 cups cauliflower florets
2 cups broccoli florets
½ cup sliced green onions
½ cup sliced black olives
½ cup sliced green olives
1/3 cup vegetable oil
¼ cup orange juice
1 tsp. grated orange peel
2 Tbsp. cider vinegar
1 tsp. dried tarragon
½ tsp. salt
½ tsp. pepper
8 cups torn salad greens

Put two inches of water in a kettle. Add cauliflower and broccoli and bring to a boil. Reduce heat, cover, and simmer for 5 to 8 minutes or until vegetables are tender, but still crisp. Rinse in cold water, drain and place in a large bowl. Add onions and olives and toss. Combine oil, orange juice, orange peel, vinegar, tarragon, salt and pepper in a jar with a tight lid; shake well. Pour over vegetable mixture and toss to coat. Refrigerate for two hours. Toss with salad greens just before serving. Serves 14 to 16.

—— Chinese Chicken Salad ——

Ingredients:

1 ½ lbs. chicken breasts or strips
1 medium head cabbage
½ cup roasted sesame seeds
1 cup sliced almonds
2 Tbsp. minced onion
1 pkg. Ramen™ noodles, crushed
 or, 1 cup chow mien noodles, crushed
½ cup rice vinegar
½ cup olive oil
2 tsp. dry mustard
½ tsp. black pepper

Bake or grill whole chicken breasts; or, cut into strips and fry in hot oil, seasoning, as desired. Cool chicken and cut into thin strips before placing in salad. Chop or cut cabbage in thin slices, then place in bowl. Add chicken, sesame seeds, almonds, onion, and noodles. Make dressing with remaining ingredients. Whisk and pour over salad ingredients, folding in to mix thoroughly. Place in refrigerator for several hours before serving.

Matt and Trina at Cee Dub and Pen's for a weekend of wood splitting and fun   Welch Photo Collection

Easy French Dressing

Ingredients:

1 tsp. salt
¼ tsp. pepper
1 tsp. paprika
1/3 cup vinegar
1 cup oil
1 clove garlic, grated or pressed

Combine all ingredients in a jar and shake well.

Words of Wisdom

When packing for a long camping trip, consider repackaging as many of your canned goods as possible in freezer bags, and freezing them before the trip. Examples to freeze are tomato sauce, refried beans, and canned vegetables. They act as ice and the freezer bags take up less space as garbage than cans do.

Ham and Cabbage Salad

Ingredients:

12 oz. cooked ham, diced
1 white or purple sweet onion, diced
1 cucumber, peeled and diced
1 green pepper, diced
2 Roma tomatoes, diced
4 cups shredded cabbage
½ cup French dressing
¼ cup mayonnaise

Put ham and vegetables in a bowl. Mix together dressing and mayonnaise in small bowl; then pour over salad ingredients. Toss lightly. Serves 8 to 10.

Fruited Chicken Salad

Ingredients:

1 ½ cups cut up chicken or turkey
1 cup fresh seedless green grapes
1 8 oz. can water chestnuts, drained and chopped
1 11 oz. can mandarin orange segments, drained
½ tsp. salt or 1 Tbsp. soy sauce
¼ tsp. curry powder, optional

Mix together in a bowl the chicken, grapes, water chestnuts, and orange segments. Mix separately remaining ingredients and toss with chicken mixture. Serves 4. Note: For a variation, cook 6 oz. elbow macaroni according to package directions and mix with other ingredients.

Carol Hampton
Bonners Ferry, Idaho

Spinach Tortellini Salad

Ingredients:

1 package tortellini
1 bag baby spinach
1 package cherry tomatoes
8 oz. sliced mushrooms
8 slices bacon, cooked and
    crumbled
½ purple onion, sliced into rings
4 oz. feta or blue cheese
1 cup ranch dressing

Cook pasta according to directions; drain, rinse, and chill. Gently toss all ingredients together in a bowl except bacon. Sprinkle bacon on top. Serve with crusty or garlic bread as a main dish or as a side salad. Serves 4 as a main and 6 as a side.

——— Honey Mustard Dressing ———

Ingredients:

½ cup honey
¼ cup Dijon mustard
¼ cup white or cider vinegar
2 Tbsp. lemon juice
1 clove garlic, minced
½ tsp. pepper
1 cup vegetable oil

Combine all ingredients, except oil, in a blender or food processor. While processing, slowly add oil in a steady stream until smooth and creamy. Store in refrigerator. Makes 2 cups.

Grandma Pen and Wyatt at the Boise Zoo 2007
Welch Photo Collection

—— Garbanzo Pasta Salad ** ——

Ingredients:

8 oz. corkscrew or bowtie pasta
2 15 oz. can garbanzo beans, rinsed and drained
½ cup chopped celery
½ cup chopped red pepper
½ cup chopped green pepper
¼ cup chopped purple onion
½ cup chopped or shredded carrots
1/3 cup red wine vinegar
4 Tbsp. mayonnaise
2 Tbsp. vegetable oil
1 Tbsp. Grey Poupon™ mustard
½ tsp. salt
½ tsp. pepper

Cook pasta according to package directions. Drain and cool. Combine pasta, garbanzo beans, celery, red and green pepper, onion, and carrots in a bowl; and toss lightly. Combine vinegar, mayonnaise, oil, mustard, salt, and pepper in a small bowl. Whisk until blended. Pour over salad ingredients, toss lightly, and serve. Serves 6. NOTES: Try substituting a can of red kidney beans for one can of garbanzo beans. Also, to make a main dish salad, add a small can of drained tuna or chicken, and a can of chopped olives.

** A photo of this recipe is featured at the beginning of the "Salads" section.

Leaf Lettuce Sweet —— Cream Dressing ——

2/3 cup whipping cream
¼ cup sugar
4 Tbsp. tarragon vinegar

Whisk cream and sugar until sugar dissolves. Add vinegar and whisk until it thickens. Pour over lettuce and serve.

Mexican Corn Salad

Ingredients:

2 cans Mexican-style corn, drained
1 green onion, sliced
1 4 oz. can diced jalapenos,
　　　drained and rinsed
1 cup mayonnaise
1 cup sour cream
1 cup grated cheddar cheese
½ small bag of Fritos™ corn chips

Mix all ingredients together except Fritos™. Crush Fritos™ and stir in just before serving.

Mike and Valerie McLain
Montrose, Colorado

Roasted Pepper Salad

Ingredients:

2 large green bell peppers
2 large red bell peppers
2 large yellow bell peppers
2 Tbsp. red wine vinegar
Salt, to taste
Fresh ground pepper, to taste
6 Tbsp. olive oil

Char whole peppers in a gas BBQ or under broiler, turning occasionally, until skins are blackened. Place hot peppers in plastic bag; let stand for about 20 minutes to steam. Peel and seed peppers, then cut into one-half inch strips and place in bowl. Mix together vinegar, salt, and pepper. Whisk in oil in a slow steady stream. Stir dressing into pepper strips. Let stand for two hours to overnight, stirring occasionally. Serve at room temperature. Serves 4 to 6.

Poppy Seed Dressing

Ingredients:

1/3 cup honey
½ tsp. salt
1/3 cup vinegar
3 Tbsp. prepared mustard
2 ½ Tbsp. poppy seed
1 ¼ cup salad oil
1 small onion, grated (optional)

Using a blender or electric mixer, add and mix ingredients in order given. Mix until oil disappears. Keeps in regrigerator up to two weeks.

Sandy Riney
Montgomery, Texas

Shrimp Salad &
Coleslaw Dressing

Ingredients:

1 ½ cups mayonnaise
½ cup white sugar
4 Tbsp. white vinegar
Salt and pepper to taste
¼ tsp. celery seed
Bay shrimp, for salad

Mix all ingredients, except shrimp, in small bowl and keep chilled. If using dressing for salad, add shrimp and dressing to salad vegetables just before serving. If using dressing for coleslaw, add to cabbage about 10 minutes before serving.

Herb Good
Hood River, Oregon

—— Spinach and Pineapple Salad ——

Ingredients:

1 pkg. baby spinach leaves
1 can pineapple rings
Feta or goat cheese chunks

Lay a bed of spinach leaves on a plate. Place pineapple rings on spinach. Top with crumbled cheese.

Sherry and Delmar Hiller
Carolyn and Danny Wheat
Hunt, Texas

—— Words of Wisdom ——

 For camp canisters, recycle square plastic containers with screw-on lids. They are nonbreakable and their shape makes packing a lot simpler.

—— Tuna Salad Deluxe ——

Ingredients:

1 large can tuna fish, drained
1 apple, cored and chopped into small pieces
1 Tbsp. diced onion
½ cup diced celery
½ cup chopped pecans
½ tsp. celery seed
½ tsp. black pepper
Mayonnaise or salad dressing to moisten

Mix all ingredients thoroughly. Stuff pita bread or spread on your favorite dark bread. Serves 4 to 6.

Sherry and Delmar Hiller
Carolyn and Danny Wheat
Hunt, Texas

Words of Wisdom

Use your home vaccuum packing system to pre-package ingredients for your camping trip menus. Your food will stay fresher longer and will take up less space in your cooler and chuck box. MAKE SURE THAT YOU LABEL EVERYTHING NOT IN THE ORIGINAL PACKAGING!

Wilted Spinach Salad

Ingredients:

3 large eggs, hardboiled, peeled and quartered
8 cups fresh baby spinach leaves
4 Tbsp. cider vinegar
1 tsp. sugar
¼ tsp. pepper
Pinch of salt
8 slices bacon, cut into 1/2" pieces
½ red onion, chopped
2 cloves garlic, minced
1 small can mandarin orange slices, drained, optional

Place washed spinach in a large bowl. In a small bowl, stir vinegar, sugar, pepper, and salt together until dissolved; set aside. Fry bacon in medium skillet over medium to high heat, until crisp. Remove bacon from skillet onto paper towels. Pour off all but 3 tablespoons of bacon drippings. Add onion and garlic to skillet and cook, stirring frequently, for about 3 minutes or slightly softened. Add vinegar mixture, then remove skillet from heat, working fast to scrape the bottom of the skillet to loosen browned bits. Pour hot dressing over spinach, add bacon, orange slices, and toss gently until spinach is slightly wilted. Arrange egg quarters on top and serve while warm.

Soups, Stews, and Chilies

Bean and Barley Chili

Ingredients:

1 large onion, chopped
2 cloves garlic, minced
2 Tbsp. olive oil
1 green pepper, chopped
1 red pepper, chopped
2 cups whole kernel corn
¾ cup quick-cooking barley
1 15 oz. can chili with beans
1 15 oz. can pinto beans, drained and rinsed
1 15 oz. can black beans, drained and rinsed
1 15 oz. can tomato sauce
1 15 oz. can diced tomatoes, undrained
1 15 oz. can vegetable or chicken broth
2 4 oz. cans diced green chilies
2 Tbsp. chili powder
½ tsp. pepper
Salt, to taste
Hot sauce, a splash or two for heat, if desired

In a 12" Dutch oven, sauté onion and garlic in olive oil for about two or three minutes, using 8-12 briquets under the Dutch oven. Stir in peppers and cook for another three or four minutes or until tender. Stir in the remaining ingredients and bring to a boil. Reduce heat by removing about one-half the briquets, cover and simmer for 15 to 20 minutes or until barley is tender. Add a salad and fresh-baked cornbread for a complete meal. Serves 8 to 10.

Steve with a S Fork of Clearwater deer at Cee Dub and Pen's in Grangeville, ID   Welch Photo Collection

Artichoke Soup

Ingredients:

2 fresh artichokes
8 cups water
3 cups split peas
1 cup lentils
1 cup cut up broccoli
2 cups cut up asparagus
2 cups mushrooms
2 cans cream of asparagus soup
2 cups chopped ham
2 Tbsp. butter or margarine
Salt and pepper to taste

Steam fresh artichokes for 45 minutes. Set out to cool. In a 12" Dutch oven or soup pot, combine remaining ingredients. Cut the artichoke hearts into small pieces and add to the soup mixture. Slow cook for 1 to 1 ½ hours.

Steve Pogue
Genesee, Idaho

Cajun Red Beans and Rice

Ingredients

2 lbs. red beans
6 slices bacon or salt pork, chopped
5 cloves garlic, minced
1 large onion, chopped
½ green pepper, chopped
2 ribs celery, chopped
1 small can tomato puree
1 Tbsp. red wine vinegar
1 Tbsp. hot sauce
2 Tbsp. Worcestershire sauce
3 bay leaves
Salt and pepper, to taste
1 lb. Cajun or smoked sausage
1 cup diced ham

Wash and soak beans over night. Drain water when ready to cook. In a large pot, cook bacon. Add garlic, onion, green pepper, celery, and cook for ten minutes. Add beans, tomato puree, vinegar, hot sauce, Worcestershire sauce, bay leaves, salt and pepper. Cover with water and bring to a boil. Add sausage and ham. Reduce heat, cover, and simmer for an hour, adding water if necessary. Remove two cups of the beans, mash them, and return them to the pot, making the texture creamy. Continue cooking slowly for at least two hours, until beans are done and the sauce is thick. Serve over rice. Serves about a dozen.

Randy Prewitt
Flavors of the ARK-LA-MISS
Monroe, Louisiana

Dill Salmon Chowder

Ingredients:

1 cup butter
½ cup all-purpose flour
1 ½ qts. chicken broth
12 oz. shredded or finely chopped dill pickles
1 cup white wine or additional chicken broth
½ medium onion, finely chopped
3 Tbsp. sugar
2 Tbsp. vinegar
1 Tbsp. dill pickle juice
3 cloves garlic, minced
1 tsp. salt
1 tsp. dill weed
1 tsp. curry powder
½ tsp. white pepper
2 bay leaves
2 cups warm milk
Dash green food coloring, optional

In a large kettle, melt butter. Add flour, cook and stir until bubbly. Gradually add broth. Add pickles, white wine or additional broth, onion, sugar, vinegar, pickle juice, garlic, salt, dill weed, curry powder, white pepper, and bay leaves; and, bring to a boil over medium heat. Reduce heat and add milk. Remove bay leaves. Add food coloring, if desired. Add large chunks of Poached Dill Mustard Salmon*. Serve hot. Also, can be served by placing chunks of the salmon in soup bowls and ladling hot soup over them.

Hobart Manns
Portland, Oregon

* Poached Dill Mustard Salmon recipe is found in the "Fish and Fowl" section.

Chippino

Ingredients:

1 cup each of green, red, and yellow bell peppers,
    coarsely chopped
2 stalks of celery, coarsely chopped
1 large sweet onion, coarsely chopped
6 cloves garlic, chopped
1 cup mushrooms, coarsely chopped
¾ to 1 lb. white fish, cut into small pieces
1 Tbsp. fresh chopped oregano
1 Tbsp. fresh chopped basil
¼ tsp. pepper
Pinch of salt
¼ cup olive oil

In a large pot, sauté the above ingredients in the olive oil until they become soft and the fish start to fall apart into small parts, then add the following:

1 large jar of chippino sauce
2 cans of Italian flavored diced tomatoes
1-2 small jars of marinated artichoke hearts,
    drain off most of oil
½ cup each of green and black olives, cut in half
1 small jar white cocktail onions, if desired

Bring all of the above to a light boil. Turn heat down and simmer for at least an hour.

Add 1 cup red wine and continue to simmer.

About 30 minutes before serving, add fresh cracked crab, fresh shrimp, fresh steamer clams, and fresh scallops. More wine can be added for taste, if desired. Let simmer until all fresh items are cooked and clams open up. Serve with hard crusty bread for dipping, and more wine.

Hobart Manns
Portland, Oregon

Words of Wisdom

Put a couple of the "flexible cutting boards" in your camp kitchen. They weigh next to nothing and take up very little space.

To make a stainless steel skillet non-stick, boil a 50/50 mixture of white vinegar and water in it every couple of weeks.

Easy Minestrone

Ingredients:

2 Tbsp. olive oil
1 medium onion, chopped
2 cloves garlic, minced
2 cans chicken broth
1 16 oz. can garbanzo beans, drained and rinsed
1 16 oz. can kidney beans, drained and rinsed
1 15 oz. can diced tomatoes
2 cups chopped kale
½ cup water
½ cup small pasta shells, uncooked
1 tsp. Italian seasoning
¼ tsp. salt
¼ tsp. crushed red pepper flakes
6 tsp. shredded Parmesan cheese

In a large saucepan or 10" Dutch oven with 6-8 briquets underneath, heat olive oil and sauté onion and garlic until onion is tender. Add the broth, beans, tomatoes, kale, water, pasta, Italian seasoning, salt, and pepper flakes. Bring to a boil. Reduce heat and cover. Simmer for 10 to 15 minutes or until pasta is tender. Sprinkle Parmesan cheese on each serving. Serves 6.

—— Four Bean Vegetarian Chili ——

Ingredients:

2 Tbsp. olive oil
1 onion, chopped
1 15 oz. can pinto beans
1 15 oz. can black beans
1 15 oz. can white beans
1 15 oz. can kidney beans
1 15 oz. can black olives, optionsl
1 16 oz. jar salsa
1 cup water
2 Tbsp. corn meal
3 Tbsp. chili powder
1 Tbsp. ground cumin
1 bunch cilantro, chopped, optional

In a large saucepan or 12" Dutch oven, heat oil and sauté onion until light brown. Add other ingredients. Stir over medium heat until well blended and heated thoroughly, or about 15 to 20 minutes. Serve immediately. Serves 6 to 8.

A gathering of members of the Riney family for dinner after hunting Nov. 2008   Welch Photo Collection

—— Green Chile Corn Chowder ——

Ingredients:

1 bunch green onions, finely diced
2 ribs celery, finely diced
1 cup roasted green chiles, coarsely chopped
1 clove garlic, finely diced
3 Tbsp. butter or margarine
3 Tbsp. flour
2 cups chicken broth
2 cups light cream or milk
5 oz. Velveeta™ light cheese, cubed
5 oz. jalapeno Monterey Jack cheese, cubed
2 small potatoes, cooked and cubed
3 carrots, cooked and diced
1 can niblets corn, drained
½ tsp. comino powder
Salt and pepper to taste

In a large sauce pan or 12" Dutch oven, saute green onions, celery, green chiles and garlic in butter or margarine. Add flour; stir to blend. Slowly add chicken broth. Whisk until blended. Stir until slightly thickened. Slowly add light cream or milk, and cubed cheese. Add potatoes, carrots, and corn. Season with comino, salt and pepper. Heat thoroughly. Serves 4 to 6.

Sherry and Delmar Hiller
Carolyn and Danny Wheat
Hunt, Texas

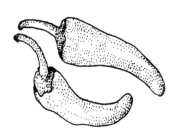

Halibut and Sweet Potato Chowder

During our northwest sportsmen's show tour, we cooks are always trying out new recipes on each other. Hobart Manns brought this recipe and it seemed to be worth trying. No one was disappointed because it was delicious! However, make it just for special events. The prices for halibut and especially the saffron makes this chowder cost prohibitive to make if you are on a budget.

Ingredients:

2 lbs. halibut, boned, skinned
1 Tbsp. olive oil
½ lb. andouille sausages,
     sliced ¼" thick
1 onion, chopped
¼ tsp. saffron threads
3 cups chicken broth
1 sweet potato, peeled,
     cut into ½" chunk
¼ cup heavy cream
Salt, to taste
Pepper, to taste
2 green onions, thinly sliced

Rinse the halibut and pat dry. Cut into chunks and set aside. Heat olive oil to medium to high in a 12" Dutch oven or large skillet. Add andouille sausage pieces and stir often until beginning to brown. Add onion and continue to stir until onion is translucent. Add the saffron, broth, and sweet potato chunks. Bring to a boil, then reduce heat and simmer until sweet potato is barely tender when pierced, about 5 minutes. Stir in the cream, salt, and pepper. Lay the chunks of halibut on top of soup, cover, and cook until halibut is opaque, but still moist-looking in the center, cutting a piece to check, or about 10 minutes. Gently stir soup. Ladle into bowl and garnish with the green onions.

— Howard's South Texas Chili ** —

Ingredients:

4 Tbsp. olive oil
6 cloves garlic, minced or sliced thin
2 lbs. flank steak, cut into 1" pieces
1 tsp. salt
½ tsp. coarse black pepper
2 large onions, diced
1 cup tomato sauce
1 cup tomato juice
1 cup tomato paste
1 cup water
½ tsp. cayenne pepper
¾ tsp. tsp. cumin
¾ tsp. oregano, or Mexican oregano
½ cup dark chili powder
5 Tbsp. flour

Set a 14" Dutch oven in the firepan with 12-16 briquets underneath. Add the olive oil, heat, and sauté the garlic for 3 to 4 minutes. Put in the meat and fry with the salt, pepper, and onions for about 10 minutes. Add the tomato sauce, juice, paste, and water. Allow to simmer for 10 to 15 minutes. Mix the remaining dry spices with the flour and slowly stir into the meat. Cook for another 1 ½ to 2 hours. The flour will thicken the chili as it cooks. Add a little water if you like it thinner. NOTE: Using ground meat, instead of flank steak, will decrease the cooking time. Serves 8 to 10 hungry hunters.

Howard Konetzke, Jr.
LaGrange, Texas

** A photo of Howard making this recipe "in a BIG way" is featured at the beginning of the "Soups, Stews, & Chilies" section.

—— Outback Angler Shrimp Soup ——

Ingredients:

¾ stick butter
1 cup finely chopped sweet onion
2/3 cup finely chopped celery
½ cup finely chopped red pepper
½ cup finely chopped green pepper
½ cup finely chopped yellow pepper
¾ cup flour
32 oz. chicken broth
8 oz. clam juice
24 oz. half and half
1 cup Chardonnay or white wine
24 oz. bloody Mary mix
¼ tsp. garlic pepper
2 Tbsp. Worcestershire sauce
 2 dashes Tabasco™ or hot pepper sauce
1 cup roasted tomato/basil marinara sauce
1 lb. freshly cooked salad shrimp

In a large pot, kettle, or 14" Dutch oven, melt butter and sauté vegetables until soft and tender. Add flour slowly, stirring constantly, to cook flour; being careful not to burn. Add chicken broth to thin out flour, stirring thoroughly. Add clam juice, half and half, wine, and Bloody Mary mix. When soup is at about medium heat, add the rest of the spices and tomato/basil marinara sauce. Add shrimp, simmer for 20 minutes, and serve.

Hobart Manns
Portland, Oregon

ABBOTT and COSTELLO

Many of us remember the humorous Bud Abbott and Lou Costello skit "Who's on first?" One of our friends emailed the following skit to us several years ago and we thought it was funny, and so appropriate for all of us that have to deal with computers. Today Abbott and Cosstello's skit might have turned out something like this:

COSTELLO CALLS TO BUY A COMPUTER FROM ABBOTT...

ABBOTT: Super Duper Computer Store. Can I help you?

COSTELLO: Thanks. I'm setting up an office in my den and I'm thinking about buying a computer.

ABBOTT: Mac?

COSTELLO: No, the name is Lou.

ABBOTT: Your computer?

COSTELLO: I don't own a computer. I want to buy one.

ABBOTT: Mac?

COSTELLO: I told you, my name's Lou.

ABBOTT: What about Windows?

COSTELLO: Why? Will it get stuffy in here?

ABBOTT: Do you want a computer with Windows?

COSTELLO: I don't know. What will I see when I look in the windows?

ABBOTT: Wallpaper.

COSTELLO: Never mind the windows. I need a computer and software.

ABBOTT: Software for Windows?

COSTELLO: No. On the computer! I need something I can use to write proposals, track expenses, and run my business. What have you got?

ABBOTT: Office.

COSTELLO: Yeah, for my office. Can you recommend anything?

ABBOTT: I just did.

COSTELLO: You just did what?

ABBOTT: Recommend something.

COSTELLO: You recommended something?

ABBOTT: Yes.

COSTELLO: For my office?

ABBOTT: Yes.

COSTELLO: OK, what did you recommend for my office?

ABBOTT: I recommend Office with Windows.

COSTELLO: I already have an office with windows! OK, let's just say I'm sitting at my computer and I want to type a proposal. What do I need?

ABBOTT: Word.

COSTELLO: What word?

ABBOTT: Word in Office

COSTELLO: The only word in office is office.

ABBOTT: The Word in Office for Windows.

COSTELLO: Which word in office for windows?

ABBOTT: The Word you get when you click the blue "W".

COSTELLO: OK, forget that! Can I watch movies on the Internet?

ABBOTT: Yes, you want Real One.

COSTELLO: Maybe a real one, maybe a cartoon. What I watch is none of your business. Just tell me what I need!

ABBOTT: Real One.

COSTELLO: If it's a long movie I also want to see reel 2, 3, and 4. Can I watch them?

ABBOTT: Of course.

COSTELLO: Great! With what?

ABBOTT: Real One.

COSTELLO: OK, I'm at my computer and I want to watch a movie. What do I do?

ABBOTT: You click the blue "1".

COSTELLO: I click the blue one what?

ABBOTT: The blue "1".

COSTELLO: Is that different than the blue w?

ABBOTT: The blue "1" is Real One and the bluer "W" is Word.

COSTELLO: What word?

ABBOTT: The Word in Office for Windows.

COSTELLO: But there's three words in "office for windows"!

ABBOTT: No, just one. But it's the most popular Word in the world.

COSTELLO: It is?

ABBOTT: Yes, but to be fair, there aren't many other Words left. It pretty much wiped out all the other Words out there.

COSTELLO: And that word is real one?

ABBOTT: Real One has nothing to do with Word. Real One isn't even part of Office.

COSTELLO: STOP! Don't start that again. What about financial bookkeeping? You have anything I can track my money with?

ABBOTT: Money.

COSTELLO: I need money to track my money?

ABBOTT: It comes bundled with your computer.

COSTELLO: What's bundled with my computer?

ABBOTT: Money.

COSTELLO: Money comes with my computer?

ABBOTT: Yes. No extra charge.

COSTELLO: I get a bundle of money with my computer? How much?

ABBOTT: One copy.

COSTELLO: Isn't it illegal to copy money?

ABBOTT: Microsoft gave us a license to copy money.

COSTELLO: They can give you a license to copy money?

ABBOTT: Why not? THEY OWN IT!

A FEW DAYS LATER…

ABBOTT: Super Duper Computer Store. Can I help you?

Breakfast line at Round Top, Texas, DO Clinic 2007
Vernon Hayes Photo

103

Hobart trying out the latest camping trailer while relaxing between his sportsmen show demos '08
Welch Photo Collection

Outback Stew

Ingredients:

2 lbs. bratwurst or Polish sausage, cut into bite-size pieces
2 lbs. red potatoes, chopped into small pieces
1 lb. baby carrots or large carrots, chopped into bite-size pieces
1 lb. celery, chopped into chunks
1 large onion, sliced into medium pieces
2 bell peppers, sliced
1 package Lipton™ Onion/Mushroom Soup mix

Add one and one-half inches of water to a 10 quart steamer pot. Place cooking basket in pot. Add in order: potatoes, carrots celery, onion, bell peppers, soup mix, and sausage. Bring to a boil over high heat. Steam cook at boil for 18 to 20 minutes, or until potatoes and carrots are cooked. Remove basket from liquid and serve. The liquid can be used later for soup stock.

Hobart Manns
Portland, Oregon

Red Beans and Rice

Ingredients:

2 cups dried red kidney beans
5 cups water, plus additional if needed
1 large onion, chopped
2 ribs celery, chopped
4 cloves garlic, minced
Salt and pepper, to taste
2 bay leaves
1 lb. Polish sausage, diced

Wash beans and soak overnight in cold water. When ready to cook, drain soaking water and place beans in large soup pot or Dutch oven. Add water and bring to boil. Reduce heat until beans are just simmering. Add onion, celery, garlic, salt, pepper, and bay leaves. Add sausage and simmer covered for about two hours or until beans are tender. If mixture is too dry, add more water. Serve over white rice or with cornbread.

Cee Dub visiting with guests at the LPR firepit 2007
Welch Photo Collection

—— Sausage and Chicken Chili ——

Ingredients:

2 Tbsp. olive oil
1 lb. bulk Italian sausage
1 lb. boneless chicken breasts or thighs, cubed
1 medium onion, chopped
2 cans Mexican-style diced tomatoes, undrained
16 oz. tomato sauce
1 15 oz. can pinto beans, drained and rinsed
1 15 oz. can black beans, drained and rinsed
1 15 oz. can kidney beans, drained and rinsed
1 15 oz. can cannellini beans, drained and rinsed
1 tsp. chili powder
½ tsp. garlic powder
¼ tsp. pepper
Hot sauce, if desired

Heat olive oil in a 12' Dutch oven, using 10-12 briquets under the DO. Crumble sausage into the DO. Add chicken pieces and onion. Cook and stir over medium heat until meat is no longer pink. Drain, if necessary. Add the remaining ingredients and stir. Cover and cook on low heat for 3 to 4 hours, using 5-6 briquets under the DO and 8-10 briquets on the lid. Change out briquets about every hour. Top each bowl of chili with a favorite grated cheese. Serves about 12.

Summer Garden Soup

Ingredients:

2 Tbsp. olive oil
1 cup chopped onion
5 cloves garlic, minced
3 cups chopped fresh tomatoes
1 cup fresh or frozen green beans
1 cup fresh or frozen peas
1 cup sliced zucchini, or
    yellow summer squash
1 Tbsp. fresh minced basil, or
    1 tsp. dried basil
1 tsp. fresh minced tarragon, or
    ¼ tsp. dried tarragon
½ tsp. fresh minced dill, or
    pinch of dill weed
½ tsp. pepper
½ tsp. salt
3 ½ cups chicken broth

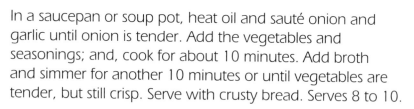

In a saucepan or soup pot, heat oil and sauté onion and garlic until onion is tender. Add the vegetables and seasonings; and, cook for about 10 minutes. Add broth and simmer for another 10 minutes or until vegetables are tender, but still crisp. Serve with crusty bread. Serves 8 to 10.

Words of Wisdom

If prepared ahead of time, potatoes and apples need to be immersed in water to keep them from turning dark due to oxidation. Try this. Before peeling or slicing, first prepare a weak salt solution of a tablespoon of salt to one-half gallon of water. Place the apple or potato slices in the solution for a couple of minutes. Drain and place in reclosable bags or snap-top containers. They will retain their color for at least twelve hours.

Tortilla Soup

Ingredients:

2 Tbsp. oil
1 medium onion, diced
3 cloves garlic, minced
1 Tbsp. chili powder
1 tsp. oregano
1 tsp. cumin, optional
1 28 oz. can crushed tomatoes
1 10.5 oz. can chicken broth
1 can water
1 green pepper, diced
1 cup whole kernel corn
½ cup lime juice
Salt and pepper, to taste
6-8 corn tortillas
2 cups grated cheese

In a soup pot or 12" Dutch oven, sauté onion and garlic in oil until soft. Stir in chili powder, oregano, and cumin. Stir in tomatoes, chicken broth, and water. Bring to a boil, cover, and simmer for a few minutes. Add green pepper, corn, and lime juice. Cover and simmer until green pepper is tender. Salt and pepper to taste. For each serving, break a tortilla into small pieces and place in a soup bowl. Ladle soup over the tortilla, sprinkle a handful of cheese on soup in each bowl, and serve. Serves 6 to 8. NOTE: Carol states that meat can be added during cooking such as chopped beef or chicken or taco meat.

Carol Hampton
Bonners Ferry, Idaho

Words of Wisdom

Don't buy potatoes that are soft or have excessive cuts, cracks, bruises, or discoloration. Avoid green potatoes because they have been exposed to light and are actually sunburned which turns the flavor bitter. You can peel or pare the green away, but if the potato is more than half green, throw it away.

When boiling potatoes for mashing, throw in a few cloves of garlic while cooking and whip them in when making mashed potatoes..

White Bean Stew

Ingredients:

1 lb. Great Northern or Navy beans
4 cups water
1 ham bone or ham hock
3 bay leaves
1 large onion, coarsely chopped
4 potatoes, peeled and cubed
4 carrots, sliced
3 cloves garlic, minced
1 tsp. thyme
1 tsp. chopped parsley
½ lb. sausage, links or bulk, cooked
Salt and pepper, to taste

Soak beans overnight in water, drain and rinse. Put beans in pot and add water, ham bone or hock, bay leaves, and onion and cook about 2 hours or until beans are tender. Remove ham bone or hock, set aside, and let cool. Add potatoes, carrots, garlic, thyme and parsley and cook until potatoes and carrots are tender. Remove meat from ham bone or hock and chop. Slice cooked sausage, if links. Add chopped ham and sausage back into soup and heat thoroughly. Add salt and pepper to taste. Remove bay leaves before serving.

White Chili

Ingredients:

1 Tbsp. oil
1 medium onion, chopped
2 cloves garlic, minced
1 15 oz. can garbanzo beans
1 15 oz. can Great Northern beans
1 lb. grilled or cooked chicken, cubed
1 14 oz can chicken broth
1 can whole kernel corn, drained
1 4 oz. can green chiles
1 tsp. cumin
1 tsp. salt
½ tsp. pepper
1 cup sour cream
½ cup heavy cream

In a large saucepan or 12" Dutch oven, heat oil and sauté onion and garlic. Add beans, chicken, broth, corn, chiles, cumin, salt, and pepper. Bring to a boil. Reduce heat and simmer 30 minutes, uncovered. Add sour cream and cream; mix thoroughly and reheat. Serves 6 to 8.

A family gathering on Thanksgiving at Cee Dub' & Pen's
Grangeville, ID   Welch Photo Collection

11/15/2008 20:06

Vegetables

Barley Risotto

Ingredients:

3 cups water
3 Tsp. chicken bouillon granules
¾ cup medium pearl barley
¼ cup finely chopped onion
1 tsp. olive oil
1 clove garlic, minced
½ cup white wine or additional water
3 Tbsp. minced fresh parsley
2 tsp. grated lemon peel
1/8 tsp. pepper
1/8 tsp. salt

In a saucepan, or 10' Dutch oven using 6-8 briquets underneath, bring water to boil. Add bouillon and stir until dissolved. Reduce heat and keep warm. In a large nonstick or cast iron skillet, cook the barley for 2 to 4 minutes, stirring until lightly browned. Place barley in a small bowl and set aside. In the same skillet, sauté onion and garlic in oil for 3 minutes until onion is tender. Stir in barley and wine or additional water. Cook and stir until all liquid is absorbed. Add heated bouillon, ½ cup at a time, stirring constantly until the liquid is absorbed between additions. Cook until barley is almost tender, about 20 minutes. Add the parsley, lemon peel, pepper, and salt; cook and stir until heated through. Serve hot. Serves 4.

Words of Wisdom

To help prevent fried foods from sticking, make sure the pan and oil are up to cooking temperature before putting food in the pan.

From the standpoint of food safety, when camping without refrigeration, utilize any leftovers within 24 hours.

— Cilantro & Lime Sweet Potatoes —

Ingredients:

2 lbs. sweet potatoes, peeled and cut into ¾" pieces
3 Tbsp. oil, divided
¾ tsp. salt, divided
¼ tsp. cayenne pepper
½ tsp. finely grated fresh lime zest
1 Tbsp. fresh lime juice
¼ cup chopped fresh cilantro

Preheat oven to 425 degrees or preheat lid of a 12" Dutch oven using 20-22 briquets on the lid. Toss sweet potatoes with 2 tablespoons oil and ¼ teaspoon salt in a shallow baking dish or DO. Arrange sweet potatoes in a single layer and roast until tender, about 25 minutes, placing the lid on the DO and using 7-8 briquets under the DO. Stir halfway through roasting. Stir together cayenne pepper, lime zest, and remaining salt in a small bowl. Add lime juice and remaining tablespoon oil and whisk together. Drizzle mixture over potatoes and sprinkle with the cilantro, stirring gently to coat potatoes. Serves 4.

—————— Creole Cabbage ——————

Ingredients:

4 slices bacon, chopped
1 small head cabbage shredded or chopped
1 purple onion, thinly sliced into rings
1 green pepper, thinly sliced into rings
1 jalapeno pepper, chopped
1 large tomato, sliced
¼ cup water
Creole seasoning, to taste

Sauté bacon in large skillet with lid or 12" Dutch oven. In layers, place the cabbage, onion, green pepper, jalapeno, and tomato over bacon. Add water, sprinkle seasoning over layers, and cover. Simmer very slowly until cabbage is clear and tender.

Fancy Brussels Sprouts

Ingredients:

1 cup water
¼ cup fresh minced parsley
2 cloves garlic, minced
1 tsp. sugar
¼ tsp. pepper
½ tsp. salt-free seasoning blend
2 pints fresh Brussels sprouts, halved; or,
    2 10 oz. packages frozen Brussels sprouts,
    thawed
8 oz. water chestnuts, drained and diced
1 Tbsp. butter or margarine

In a saucepan over medium heat, bring water, parsley, garlic, sugar, and seasonings to a boil. Add Brussels sprouts. Cover and simmer for 6 to 8 minutes or until tender; drain. Add water chestnuts and butter or margarine and heat through. Makes 6 servings.

Fancy Red Potatoes

Ingredients:

2 lbs. small red potatoes, or
    cut into bite-size pieces
1/3 cup olive oil
2 Tbsp. crushed red peppers
2 Tbsp. minced garlic
Fresh chopped herbs, optional,
    (such as dill, parsley, rosemary, basil)

Put potatoes in a 12 inch Dutch oven. Add oil and toss. Add remaining ingredients and stir to coat potatoes. Cover and bake using 8-10 briquets under the oven and 18-20 on the lid. Check after 20 minutes and add one-half cup water, if necessary. Bake about 40 minutes or until potatoes are tender.

Fried Rice

Ingredients:

1 cup uncooked rice
1 egg, beaten
Pinch of salt
Pinch of sugar, optional
Splash of soy sauce, optional
2 cloves garlic, chopped
Frozen veggies, chopped, if desired
Meat, cut into small pieces
Bean sprouts
2 tsp. oil
1 tsp. sugar

Place rice in container and wash with water three times. Put rice in kettle and cover with water double the rice depth. Boil with the lid cocked off. When water boils out, turn heat to warm. Cover and let cook for approximately 3 minutes, not allowing rice to dry out. Remove rice to bowl. Mix in beaten egg, salt, sugar, and soy sauce. Set aside. Place the garlic, veggies, meat, and bean sprouts, in separate containers. Heat oil in a frying pan. Add sugar and cook until a brown color appears; then add the garlic. Next add meat and brown. Next add veggies and cook until nearly done. Add rice and cook until done, stirring constantly.

Matt Dykas
Boise, Idaho

Matt and Wyatt
dressed in their
flight jackets
December 2007
Welch Photo
Collection

Joel's Brown White Rice

Ingredients:

1 cup white rice
2 cups beef consommé
1 onion, chopped
2 cups mushrooms, sliced
1/3 stick butter

Melt butter in a 10" Dutch oven. Add rice and brown. Add onions and mushrooms and mix with the rice. Cover with consommé. Put on DO lid. Bake at 350 degrees for 1 hour and 20 minutes, using 5 briquets under the oven and 14-16 on the lid; or, bake at 375 degrees for 1 hour, using 6 briquets under the oven and 16-18 on the lid. Serves 4.

Joel Walton
Julian, California

Joel and Rich Walton attended one of our Dutch Oven University Clinics at our home in Grangeville, Idaho. The next year Joel and Rich visited during deer season for Joel to get in a little hunting. During that visit Joel prepared this rice dish for us one evening. It was simple, yet so delicious. He also prepared a salad and beef prepared in Joel's Bourbon Teriyaki Marinade along with the rice to complete the meal. Joel's Bourbon Teriyaki Marinade recipe is in the Sauces, Marinades, and Rubs section of this cookbook. The rice and beef entreés go very well together.

Joel cooking his rice and beef entrees for dinner at Cee
Dub and Pen's during fall deer hunt Nov. 2005
Walton Photo Collection

Monterey Jack and
———— Green Chile Rice ————

Ingredients:

1 cup white rice, uncooked
2 cups water
1 Tbsp. butter or margarine
1 cup Monterey Jack cheese, grated
1 cup sour cream
1 4 oz. can diced green chiles; or,
    the equivalent of fresh roasted green
    chiles, diced

Cook the rice in the water until water is absorbed.
While rice is hot, stir in the remaining ingredients. Heat
uncovered for about 10 minutes, or until mixture bubbles.
Serves 4.

Sherry and Delmar Hiller
Carolyn and Danny Wheat
Hunt, Texas

A THIEF IN THE NIGHT

  The theft occurred about 2:30 in the morning on a bright moonlit night at a camp along Mahogany Creek in the Upper Pahsimeroi Valley of central Idaho in September of 1981. A couple of months previously, a computer had drawn my name as one of the first eight lucky souls to draw a bighorn sheep tag for what is popularly known as the Mt. Borah unit. A buddy and I pitched our camp in a little meadow alongside the creek where there were some fairly good grass for our two horses. Doing the leg work of getting part way up the hills each morning were two of my horses. Sam, a palomino quarter horse mare, had a pretty easy job of packing my buddy Al around; and, Lewis, a mixed blood sorrel gelding who was stout enough to pack someone twice my size, ended up with my Hamley saddle on his back each morning.

  When I say Lewis was a good-sized horse, folks who know about such things will tell you that any pony that wears number two shoes is a big animal. A standard-sized halter would fit on his head, but when buckled on the last notch effectively kept him from opening his mouth. Horses are just like folks; we all have our quirks, some more than others. Lewis fell in the "some more than others" category. There would be days when if he saw his shadow he would shy sideways and leave me grabbing for leather. A rattlesnake or a hippy backpacker brought on a wide-eyed, snot-blowing fit. But worst of all, he was scared of blood… not good for a game warden's horse. Most horses can be broken of such dislikes by putting them in a corral with water and place their ration of oats on a green deer or elk hide. Not Lewis! He'd stand in that corral as far from that green hide as he could get until his ribs started showing. But for all his faults, his good points kept him in my string for over fifteen years till old age forced me to retire him.

  Of his good traits, the one that kept him employed for so long was that Lewis just liked to be around people.

In fact it was like having a 1,400 pound Labrador retriever who is always underfoot. When setting up a camp I always left my stock tied for awhile after unloading them and brushing them down. Once they settled down after a day's work, I gave them a little sweet feed under the picket line. Some horses need to be hobbled and bells hung around their necks to help keep them honest and accessible when the time came to go back to work, but not Lewis. He'd hang around camp to the point he sometimes made a nuisance of himself. On his own, Lewis never quit me in all the years and miles we spent together, except for one time when he was led astray by a certain palomino mare…but that's another story!

Most folks who've spent much time camping know the aggravation of finding that a critter or two had helped themselves to grub left laying around or in unsecured coolers. In my case I've suffered the depredations of mice and chipmunks. And one time on a float trip on the Yampa River, finding that a rock chuck had helped himself to a brick of cheese left out after lunch. I quickly learned to hang my saddles up beyond the reach of porcupines after having a saddle latigo and a couple of cinches chewed in two for the salt from the stock's sweat.

Occasionally, circumstances beyond our control may allow us to witness events we normally wouldn't be present for; and, in my case it was the theft of a dozen Red Delicious apples. On the night in question the circumstances included a nice warm sleeping bag, a very cold night, and a bladder that was increasingly distended. I put off crawling out of my sleeping bag as long has humanly possible. I eased the door of the wall tent open quietly to avoid waking Al when I saw Lewis engaged in an act of larceny. He was kneeling on his front legs with his head inside a brown grocery bag munching apples that was underneath my camp table. My camp table was nothing more than one-half a 4' x 8' foot sheet of plywood ripped lengthwise supported by two pack boxes. On that table was my camp stove, lantern, coffee pot, dishes, etc., etc. I knew that if I startled Lewis he would become unglued and stand up. The thought of his scattering my whole kitchen kept me standing there shivering in my skivvies unable to laugh or pee! When the last apple was devoured, he very adroitly backed up on his knees and stood up. With a loud smack of his lips, he ambled off not knowing I had caught him red-hoofed, so to speak.

My maniacal and much relieved laughter brought Al up out of a very sound sleep. When I told him the story we both laughed so long and loud we couldn't get back to sleep. We just got up and drank a pot of coffee by moonlight and visited until time to grain the horses and saddle up for the day's hunt.

PS: Though we saw a lot of sheep, I never pulled the trigger. I ended up putting my tag in a skillet with a can of mushroom soup and called it "Sheep Hunt 1981"!

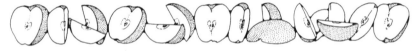

Southfork of Clearwater deer camp at Cee Dub & Pen's near Grangeville, ID Nov. 2005   Joe Turner Photo

Pen's Fried Cabbage

Ingredients:

1 lb. bacon, diced
1 large onion, diced or chopped
4 cloves garlic, minced
1 head cabbage, chopped
1 tsp. salt
¾ tsp. pepper
1 Tbsp. sugar
¼ cup vinegar

In a large skillet, fry bacon until nearly cooked. Add onion and garlic and continue to sauté, stirring frequently, until onions are translucent. Add cabbage and remaining ingredients. Continue to fry, turning with spatula. Fry to desired consistency. Can serve as a main or as a side dish with breakfast, lunch, or dinner. Serves 6 to 8.

Penny Welch
Mountain Home, Texas

Taking Scooter and Rosie for a ride around the ranch
Summer 2008   Welch Photo Collection

Rice and Veggies

Ingredients:

2 Tbsp. butter
1 small onion, chopped
½ cup chopped celery leaves
1 rib celery, chopped
1 lb. mushrooms, sliced
3 cups instant rice, uncooked
3 cups water
4 tsp. Greek seasoning
½ cup chopped pecans, optional

In a large saucepan, or 10" Dutch oven with 6-8 briquets underneath, melt butter and sauté onion, celery leaves, and celery for about 3 to 5 minutes. Add mushrooms and sauté for 3 to 5 minutes longer. Add rice, and continue to cook for another 3 to 5 minutes or until lightly brown. Stir in the water and seasoning. Bring to a boil. Remove from heat, cover, and let stand for 5 minutes. Fluff with a fork and sprinkle with pecans, if desired. Serves 8.

Sesame Asparagus

Ingredients:

1 lb. fresh asparagus, trimmed and cut into 2" pieces
1 tsp. sesame oil
¼ tsp. salt
¼ tsp. pepper
½ tsp. toasted sesame seeds

Place asparagus in a saucepan and add water. Cook asparagus for about six minutes or until tender, but still crisp; drain. Add sesame oil, salt, and pepper. Gently stir to coat asparagus. Place in serving bowl and sprinkle sesame seeds over the asparagus and serve. Serves 4.

Snappy Sugar Snap Peas

Ingredients:

1 lb. fresh or frozen sugar snap peas
½ cup water
1 Tbsp. butter or margarine
2 cloves garlic, minced
¾ tsp. lemon-pepper seasoning
½ tsp. salt

In a skillet or saucepan, bring peas and water to a boil. Reduce heat, cover and simmer for 6 minutes or until tender. Drain and add the remaining ingredients. Cook, stirring frequently, for 2 to 3 minutes until well coated. Makes 4 servings.

Onion Rings

Ingredients:

1 large sweet onion
1 quart buttermilk
2 cups flour
Cooking oil

Thickly slice onion and separate into rings. Cover with buttermilk and let stand for one hour. Put flour in plastic or paper bag. Add onion rings, inflate bag, and shake until rings are coated with flour. Fry in hot oil and drain on paper towels.

——— Wrapped Green Beans ** ———

Ingredients:

2 cans whole cut green beans
¾-1 cup roasted raspberry chipotle sauce
½ lb. sliced bacon

Drain green beans and place in resealable bag. Add raspberry sauce to green beans. Marinate for at least two hours in the refrigerator. Pour out into a bowl. Cut bacon strips in half. Lay out a bacon strip. Lay several marinated green beans on the strip of bacon. Wrap the bacon around the green beans and secure with a toothpick. Place bundles in 13 x 9 inch baking dish or 12 inch Dutch oven. Drizzle any excess marinade over the bundles. Bake in the oven uncovered at 325 degrees for 30 to 40 minutes until bacon looks cooked and slightly crispy; or, in covered DO using 6-8 briquets under the oven and 18-22 on the lid. NOTES: Other flavors of dressings can be used such as French or Italian. Can make with asparagus spears.

Sandy Riney
Montgomery, Texas

** A photo of this recipe is featured at the beginning of the "Vegetables" section.

Pen and Emmett at a jam session at *LPR*
Welch Photo Collection

124

Vernon Hayes Photo

Marinades, Sauces, & Rubs

Basic BBQ Rub **

Ingredients:

Diamond Crystal Kosher Salt™; or,
 1/3 less Morton® Kosher Salt
White granulated sugar
Dark chili powder
Canadian or Montreal Steak Seasoning™
Pinch of cayenne or chipotle for heat, to taste,
 optional

Measure out equal parts by volume. Start with 2 tablespoons of each ingredient. Use on beef, pork, chicken, turkey, and as a table condiment. NOTE: Paint meat with a thin coat of brown mustard prior to applying rub; the rub will stick easier to the meat, but the mustard will not effect the taste. NOTE: The basic rub works very well, but for a Southwest flavor, add equal portions of ground cumin and Mexican oregano to the rub mixture.

Konrad and Phyllis Haskins
Teddy Bear BBQ
Duvall, Washington

** A photo using this recipe is featured at the beginning of the "Sauces, Marinades, and Rubs" section.

Beef Kabob Marinade

Ingredients:

½ cup soy sauce
½ cup cooking oil
2 tsp. sugar
¼ cup orange juice
1 tsp. ginger

Mix all ingredients and place in resealable bag. Add about one pound of beef cut into chunks. Marinate for an hour.

Cocktail Sauce

Ingredients:

Ketchup
Horseradish, to taste
Lemon juice, to taste
Worcestershire sauce, to taste, optional

Mix ingredients and chill. Use as dipping sauce for shrimp, oysters, scallops, chicken strips, or finger steaks.

Herb Good
Hood River, Oregon

Quick Tartar Sauce

Ingredients:

1 cup mayonnaise
1 Tbsp. dill relish
1 Tbsp. sweet relish
2-3 Tbsp. chopped onions
1 squeeze lemon juice
Salt and pepper, to taste
Worcestershire sauce, to taste, optional
Garlic powder, to taste, optional

Mix all ingredients and chill. Serve with deep fried fish or use as a spread on fish sandwiches.

Herb Good
Hood River, Oregon

Easy BBQ Sauce

Ingredients:

½ cup Heinz™ ketchup
¼ cup lime juice
¼ cup soy sauce
¼ cup honey

Mix all ingredients and chill. Great for basting on BBQ.

Pam Harris
Lewiston, Idaho

Denton's Breading

Members of the Perkins clan came to visit us in Idaho a couple times each year to turkey hunt and deer hunt. Young Denton was always a very picky eater and subsisted on minimal amounts of food during the visits. On one of our visits through Utah, we saw Denton and his family. His mom and dad informed is that if ANY food was cooked with his breading recipe on it, he would eat it; so we had him write down his "special" recipe for this cookbook.

Ingredients:

½ box snack crackers
½ sleeve saltines
1 ½-2 cups flour
2 Tbsp. cornmeall
1 tsp. salt
1 tsp. pepper
1 tsp. Cajun seasoning
½ tsp. seasoned salt

Crush crackers and mix all ingredients together. Fill frying pan with cooking oil. Put meat pieces in water or egg yolk to make the breading stick to the meat. Then roll the meat in the breading. Fry until brown.

Denton Perkins
St. Anthony, Idaho

———— Chef's Salt ————

Shari told us that her mother-in-law used this recipe as an all-purpose seasoning that she always kept on hand.

Ingredients:

1 cup salt
1 Tbsp. paprika
1 tsp. fresh ground black pepper
½ tsp. white pepper
¼ tsp. celery salt
¼ tsp. garlic salt (not powder)

Mix well and keep in jar.

Shari Truitt
Hunt, Texas

Bryant and Shari Truitt at one of Cee Dub's DO Clinics
Hunt, Texas November 2006   Truitt Photo Collection

———— Jezebel Sauce ————

Ingredients:

1 10 oz. jar apple jelly
1 10 oz. jar pineapple preserves
1 5 oz. jar horseradish
1 5 oz. jar mustard, optional

Mix jelly, preserves, horseradish, and mustard together in a blender or with a fork. Serve with ham. Stores well in refrigerator in closed container.

Shari Truitt
Hunt, Texas

Sitting down to dinner during fall hunting season
Grangeville, Idaho Fall 2005   Welch Photo Collection

Joel's Bourbon
——————— Teriyaki Marinade ———————

Ingredients:

2/3 cup Kikkoman Teriyaki™ sauce
1 1/3 cups water
4 Tbsp. sugar
½ tsp. ginger
2 oz. bourbon
4 cloves garlic, minced

For beef, use chuck, top sirloin, or London broil.
Marinade can also be used for chicken or turkey.
Cube 2 pounds of meat into 1 ½ inch chunks and set
aside. Combine other ingredients, mixing thoroughly. Add
meat. Marinade for 8 to 12 hours, turning occasionally.
Cook chunks on the grill or put meat on skewers and
grill. Can also place meat on a bed of onions in a 12"
Dutch oven, cover, and cook for 1 ½ to 2 hours, using
5-7 briquets under the oven and 16-18 briquets on the
lid. Serve with Joel's Brown White Rice in the Vegetables
section. Serves 4 to 6.

Joel Walton
Julian, California

——— Salmon Teriyaki Marinade ———

Ingredients:

¾ cup teriyaki marinade or sauce
2 Tbsp. packed brown sugar
1 tsp. fresh grated ginger root
4 salmon steaks, ¾" thick

Combine the sauce, brown sugar, and ginger. Remove ¼ cup of the mixture and reserve. Place steaks in large plastic resealable bag and pour remaining mixture over steaks. Press air out of bag and close bag securely. Turn bag over several times to thoroughly coat steaks. Marinade for 30 minutes to an hour. Grill or broil steaks about 4 minutes on each side, or until fish flakes easily with fork. Brush on reserved sauce while cooking. NOTE: This marinade also works well with white fish. Serves 4.

Brian cooking salmon on a river trip in Idaho 2007

B Welch Photo

Hillbilly,
Cookin'

HILLBILLY COOKIN'

I found the following definition for "Hill Billy" in my Revised Edition of Webster's Pocket Dictionary. "hillbilly n. person who lives in a remote area." (By that definition I and a lot of other folks fall into that category.) Anyway... the original idea for and the initial recipes in this section came from three friends of mine I call the Horsehoe Bend Hill Billies. Actually they call themselves "hill billies" and since they are friends of mine I added the name of their home town of Horseshoe Bend, Idaho, in order to distinguish them from other hill billies. Horseshoe Bend is a small town along the Payette River in Idaho, about a thirty minute drive north of Boise, the capitol city.

Steve Asher, Chuck Byers, and Steve Pogue have spent nearly their entire adult lives working in the timber industry. Asher is a timber faller, Pogue a log truck driver, and Byers a cat skinner/skidder/loader operator. Traffic jams seldom occur as they commute to work over gravel and old forest roads. When they look up they only see towering Ponderosa Pines, Lodgepole Pines, Douglas Fir, Grand Fir, and White Fir instead of office towers built of glass and steel. So, though they live in a small town they work in remote areas on a daily basis. By nature loggers are very resourceful folks. When a need arises out in the woods the old saying that "necessity is the mother of invention" definitely holds true.

If a logging operation has a social center, it is at the log landing. It's here that the logs are skidded out of the woods where the loader operator stacks them in decks so they can be loaded onto trucks for transport to a mill. At days end the fallers come out of the woods to the landing where the operators and truck drivers are fueling the machinery for the next day's operations. Especially during colder weather there is always a warming fire burning at the edge of the landing. Typically someone opens a cooler full of cold malted beverages and passes them around while the guys "shoot the bull" about what went on during the day before heading back to their travel trailers and wall tents at the logging camp. We hope you enjoy their recipes that fit into the "Hill Billy" category!

—————— Shovel Steak ——————

Put a little cooking oil on a shovel over the fire and fry steaks with fried onions.

Steve Pogue
Genesee, Idaho

—————— Pogue's Flat Rock Salmon ——————

Find a flat rock about 14 inched long, about 6 or 7 inches wide and 2 or 3 inches thick. Build a fire ring and set flat rock across top of fire ring rocks above hot coals. When flat rock is good and hot, place salmon steak skin side down on rock. Salmon steak cooks itself in its own oil. Of course, cooking time varies according to heat from your fire. This works excellent on the river bank with the salmon you just caught.

—— "Bobwire" Fence Finger Steaks ——

Hang finger steaks on the 2nd wire down from the top of a four-strand fence and build a fire underneath. Use your own judgment and adjust distance from fire, if necessary. Cook about 5 to 7 minutes.

Steve Pogue
Genesee, Idaho

Steve helping Cee Dub in Hayden, Idaho with a Dutch
Oven cooking demo   Welch Photo Collection

Below are two hillbilly entrees that Cee Dub prepared
during his sportsman show tour in the Northwest in 2007.
They are "Steak on a Rake" and "Pitchfork Kabobs"
                              Welch Photo Collection

BYERS BEER CAN CHICKEN

Chuck Byers came up with this recipe on a log landing near Deadwood Reservoir in the Boise National Forest on a cold October afternoon. It all started when a ruffed grouse wandered up onto the landing as the crew stood around the warming fire. Since grouse season was open Chuck reached into the cab of his skidder and pulled out a .22 pistol kept for just such opportunities. With grouse in hand Chuck came back to the fire where he set about making a quick snack with what he had on hand. First he filleted the breast meat off the grouse and cut off the legs and thighs. Next he took an empty 12 oz. beer can and with a sharp pocket knife made a vertical cut from the top to the bottom starting near the pop top opening. Then he made two horizontal cuts off his original cut on both the top and bottom which created a set of clam shell doors. (See Photos) To finish his beer can cooker he carefully reached inside the can and pushed the pop top closed. After seasoning the grouse breasts and legs with salt and pepper from his lunch pail he placed the meat inside the beer can and pressed the doors closed. He raked a small bed of coals away from the fire and placed them around his beer can. In about thirty minutes he pulled the coals away from the can and opened the doors. His grouse was done perfectly.

We've modified Chuck's original recipe to use a chicken breast. It's best to wear a pair of gloves when cutting the beer or soda can as the edges are quite sharp. Also, for the bigger appetite, one can use larger beer cans! With 32 oz. cans we've cooked kraut and dogs using bratwurst.

> 1 12 oz. beer or soda can with clam shell doors already cut and pop top pressed shut
> 1 small chicken breast
> 1Tbsp. chopped green onion
> 1 Tbsp. Parmesan cheese
> Salt and pepper

Season the chicken breast with salt and pepper. Place breast in beer can and sprinkle green onions and Parmesan cheese over the top. Press doors shut. Place three briquets on each side and cook for 30-40 minutes.

Byers Beer Can Chicken just off the fire and ready to eat! Spring 2007 Welch Photo Collection

Chuck Byers having a successful whitetail hunt in 2005 Welch Photo Collection

═ WHAT MAKES A GOOD COOK? ═

In the twelve years since I published my first cookbook, I've become a better cook. Now conventional wisdom would say it's a 'no brainer' that improvement comes with practice. Most cooks I know would agree with that. The old cliché "Practice Makes Perfect" probably in the case of cooks should really be "Practice Brings Us Closer To Perfection"! But, in my mind, though, two other things have also contributed to my becoming a better cook.

My best guess is that in the years since that first cookbook hit the shelves, I've driven over a quarter million miles either headed to our next cooking gig or coming home from a clinic or cooking gig. Many a mile have passed as Pen and I either talked for hours about what we'd just done; or, ways to make the next gig on the horizon a little better.

But, in my case the one thing I know that has helped me edge a little closer to "perfection" is teaching Dutch oven cookin'! When Pen and I started teaching Dutch oven cookin' clinics, I would start with a different group of students every time. Clinics quickly became a routine where I used the same recipes time after time, and my narrative during the class became boring to the only person besides myself that attended every clinic, Pen, my wife.

Change was forced upon me back in 2003 when I pulled into Ozona, Texas, again, to teach a clinic for a bunch of West Texas cowboys. Half of the folks signed up had taken the clinic in Ozona the previous year, and I knew it wouldn't make much of an impression on them if I repeated verbatim what we'd done the year before. So, as my wife so aptly puts it, it was time to s-t-r-e-t-c-h.

The day before the clinic found me standing in front of the fax machine at the Middle School waiting for Pen to fax me some new recipes from home in Idaho. When the fax machine quit spitting out recipes, I humped up a little knowing that a couple of them would be a stretch for me, let alone teaching them to others. But, two days later when the clinic wrapped up, I realized teaching something new, although it increased my own stress level, it also made me put more into my teaching. As a cook and teacher I now look forward to challenges, whether it is new recipes, or teaching folks who find what we do of enough value to come back to clinics for seconds or thirds!

— Coffee Can Birds and Wild Rice —

Cut into small chunks 5 or 6 quail breasts or 2 grouse breasts, and put in a coffee can. Add mushrooms and rice. Add some liquid such as beer or water. Cook on an open fire. Set can close to coals or on a grate above the fire.

Steve Pogue
Genesee, Idaho

—— Under the Hood Cooking ——

When you are going hunting, take along the leftovers from dinner the previous night such as tamales or meat or pizza, and wrap in tin foil. For lunch set on the motor of your pickup and road hunt for one hour on a motor at 175 degrees. After one hour, park in a wide spot along the road, grab another cold beer and open the hood of the ol' pickup and have a warm lunch. You can't cook on a motor, but a motor is great for warming up food. I've eaten a lot of burritos, pizza, and my favorite, polish sausage in a bun with sauerkraut, off a motor on a log loader or logging truck.

Steve Pogue
Genesee, Idaho

THE LETTER

When we began to get serious about writing another cookbook, we asked friends and family members to send us recipes. We received the letter below, supposedly from Steve Asher, one of our loggin' buddies. Although we soon realized the letter was NOT from Steve, it could have been! He is truly Unique.Anyway, we had a good laugh, but decided to go ahead and put the letter in the cookbook. Of course, the recipe has never been tried!

Welch,

Pogue told me you were lookin' for some new resapee's for your new cook book. So I am sendin' you a good @#$#*&% one.

12-18 meadow lark breasts
Some %#$@*&% mushrooms (Morels are the best.)
Some Rice
And some %#$@&*% aspergrass
One can of mushroom soup

fillet meat off the %$&@#%& meadow larks and throw in the blankety-blank pot with the son of a bitchen soup, aspergrass and the &%$#&*# rice. Then cook it tell it gets done.
This resapee works good with yellow warblers two. I even %$#@&%# tried it with perigrine falcon. Cant wait to see this resapee in your new %$#@&%# cook book.

Signed

Steve Asher

NOTE: This recipe was beyond the capabilities of ANY nutritional analysis program!

Don Elliott Photo

Sausage

WHY MAKE YOUR OWN ══ SAUSAGE AND BURGER ? ══

I can't think of anything that I buy in the store that is as good as what I can make myself at home. Sausage and burger are not exceptions to that rule. In no way am I trying to write a definitive volume on home sausage making. I'm merely trying to share our experiences and make the learning curve a little less steep.

Much of my and Pen's philosophy regarding food traces back to the way we were raised in Southern Idaho in the 1950's and 60's. Both our families depended on produce from the garden as well as beef, pork, lamb, and poultry raised on our own places. My family also put up venison and fish as well.

As little kids, butchering day ranked pretty close to the calendar holidays as something we both looked forward to. It was a family event. Each person, no matter how young, had a job that was essential to the whole operation. What was stored in our freezers and fruit cellars saved many a trip to the grocery store! What we didn't realize at the time was instead of being poor; we were early trendsetters in the "organically grown" movement! (It took us about forty years to come to that conclusion.)

Anyway...making your own sausage and burger yields a healthier and fresher product to put on the table. In a way, you are more in control of your own destiny. You can cut the fat and salt; and season it to your own personal taste. You actually end up with sausage that tastes better than store-bought and is much healthier for you and your family.

When we lived in Idaho, we made all our burger and sausage from deer and elk. Since we've moved to Texas we utilize wild hog for our sausage and deer meat for burger. But, if you prefer not to use game meat; or, it's not available to you, you can purchase everything you need at the grocery store and still spend less per pound on any given product. For example, you can often find pork shoulders or pork butts on special for about $1.10 to $1.25 per pound. De-bone and trim as much of the fat off as you want, and you have the fixin's for some great breakfast sausage.

For beef sausage and burger, try to find a wholesale meat outfit or grocery store that will sell "boxed meat" right off the truck to you. You'll essentially be buying in case lot quantities, but the price per pound will be a pleasant surprise compared to the per pound price in the butcher's case. Ask for shoulder clods, beef knuckles, and top rounds. All three cuts require very little trimming of fat and make great burger and beef-based sausage. If you want to make your own beef jerky, too, try the inside top rounds. They are the preferred cut for most commercial jerky operations. Besides being very lean, they have very little connective tissue.

Words of Wisdom

For a different flavor when grilling sausages such as Bratwurst, German or Breakfast, try simmering them first in apple juice for a few minutes

HOW WE GOT STARTED
MAKING SAUSAGE

In the late 1990's Pen and I first got into making our own home-made sausage. Two things fueled our interest. First, was a surplus of meat when some friends gave us an elk one fall. Between the two of us, we'd already put four deer in the freezer which had already yielded us a year's supply of burger. Secondly, we'd started making home-made sauerkraut a couple of years earlier which had fueled an increase in our buying more store-bought sausage to cook with the kraut. With the help of a friend who owned a meat processing facility and sold his own brand of sausage to local stores, we got the fixin's we needed to get started.

On New Years Eve 1999, while the rest of the world was worrying about Y2K, Pen and I had our first sausage party. That day there was just the two of us, but since then we've turned it into a family event. Anyway…we actually started the party the day before when we took the boneless elk meat to a friend who had a 2 hp commercial grinder. After we added 10% pork fat and 10% lean pork by weight, we ended up with about two hundred pounds of coarse ground meat. Our seasonings were for twenty-five pound batches so we started by weighing the meat and putting it in our largest bowls and big plastic tubs. It was pretty cold so after adding the seasonings we folded the back seat down in Pen's Grand Cherokee Jeep, and held them there until we were ready to stuff and package them. If memory serves me correctly we made the following kinds and amounts that day.

> Breakfast – 50 lbs
> Bratwurst – 50 lbs
> German – 25 lbs
> Polish – 25 lbs
> Italian – 25 lbs
> Hound Dogs – 25 lbs (This is actually just seasoned burger stuffed in a casing.)

We started by mixing our dry seasonings in each tub of meat and mixing it by hand. After thoroughly mixing it, we would set the tubs in the Jeep and let the meat with the seasonings and spices rest for awhile. We would re-mix each batch a couple of times to make sure the spices and seasonings were well blended.

Using our hand-crank grinder we started by running the breakfast sausage though the fine grind plate. This we packaged in bulk packages of approximately 1 ½ pounds. The remaining one hundred and fifty pounds were run through the fine grind plate and stuffed in natural hog casings via a stuffing tube on the front of the grinder.

It was after 10:00 pm when we finished. My arms and back felt like I'd split and stacked two cords of wood.

What ended up being the funny part of the whole operation was Penny's Jeep smelled like a delicatessen for about two months.

We've since refined our methods and techniques and hope what you read in this section will get you on your way to making your own delicious sausage. Please feel free to experiment with our recipes

---

Breakfast Sausage

Ingredients:

25 lb. meat (pork, beef, venison, or combination),
    cut into 1 1/2 " cubes or strips, and chilled
3/4 cup dried onions, minced or diced
5 Tbsp. fresh rosemary, finely chopped
2 Tbsp. garlic powder
3 Tbsp. black pepper
2 Tbsp. paprika
3 Tbsp. salt
1 Tbsp. ginger
1 Tbsp. nutmeg
1 Tbsp. dry mustard
2 Tbsp. crushed red pepper
1 Tbsp. sage
1 Tbsp. ground thyme
2 cups water

ROSEMARY

Place meat in a large tub. Mix all the other ingredients except water in a bowl. Add water and mix thoroughly. Pour seasoning mixture over cold meat in tub and mix until meat is coated. Place in refrigerator for a minimum of 3 to 4 hours; overnight is better. Occasionally mix and turn seasoned meat to distribute seasoning throughout the meat. Run the meat through a grinder into a separate container. Package into bags, label, and freeze.

Andouille Sausage

The origin of Andouille pork sausage is in and around New Orleans, Louisiana. This spicey Cajun sausage makes a tasty grilled sausage appetizer, a delicious sausage wrap, as well as an integral ingredient in gumbo. We recently became aware of this tasty sausage while in Louisiana; and decided to attempt to develop a recipe so that we could enjoy this sausage on a regular basis for a fraction of the cost of the store-bought variety. We are excited to share our results with you!

Ingredients:

10 lbs. meat (pork, beef, venison, or combination),
    cut into 1 1/2" cubes or strips, and chilled
½ cup minced garlic
2 Tbsp. salt
1 Tbsp. black pepper
1 tsp. ground thyme
2 Tbsp. paprika
1 tsp. crushed bay leaves
½ tsp. sage
1 tsp. cayenne
3 Tbsp. liquid smoke
1 tsp. chili powder
1 tsp. nutmeg
1 tsp. mace
1 beer or 12 oz. water

Place meat in a large tub. Mix all the other ingredients except water in a bowl. Add water and mix thoroughly. Pour seasoning mixture over cold meat in tub and mix until meat is coated. Place in refrigerator for a minimum of 3 to 4 hours; overnight is better. Occasionally mix and turn seasoned meat to distribute seasoning throughout the meat. Run the meat through a grinder into casings. Twist into links and snip into individual sausages. Package into bags, label, and freeze.

RATIO OF FAT TO MEAT

For the first several years that we did our own sausage and burger, we mixed 10% each by weight of lean pork and pork fat to our venison. This was our basic grinding mix. We would package some of this after the coarse grind for chili meat, and the remainder would be run through the grinder's fine plate for sausage or regular hamburger. At approximately 10% fat, this is a fairly austere mix when compared to the fat content of store-bought burger and sausage. We found when frying this, we needed to add a dab of cooking oil to the skillet to get started. When browning burger for tacos, we never needed to drain excess oil off the meat. This made a great grinding mixture, but buying the boneless pork and pork fat added quite a bit to our costs.

One time we experimented and did a small batch of burger with no fat added. It tasted OK but it was really dry! An old college roommate, river running buddy, and occasional hunting pardner, Tom Beck, and his wife, Sandy, of Dolores, Colorado passed on to us a combination that works well for them. Before their initial coarse grind for each ten pounds of well-trimmed venison, they chop and add a three pound package of bacon ends and pieces. We decided to give it a try and liked not only the taste but the lower price because we bought the bacon on special.

Based on the label information on the bacon package, we determined the fat content to be approximately 50%. This computes out to a fat content of approximately 13% for our basic grinding mix. We use this for burger which makes every hamburger a bacon burger, and gives a little extra spin to the different sausage we make from it. By comparison, a package of store-bought sausage someone left in our freezer shows a total fat content of about 43%. It is a no brainer as to which is the healthier sausage!

SAUSAGE MAKING - TRADITIONAL METHOD

Making sausage in the traditional way includes several steps. In order, they are coarse grinding the meat, mixing in the desired seasonings, letting the meat rest to allow the seasonings to penetrate the meat, re-grinding the meat through a fine plate, and packaging the finished product. This becomes a rather labor intensive process, especially if your're grinding large amounts of meat.

A typical coarse grind results when using a grinding plate with holes of approximately 3/8" diameter. As is, this makes great chili meat, but is a bit too coarse for sausage and hamburger.

We recommend dissolving the dry seasonings in a liquid. Usually we use water, but depending on the recipe, we may use milk or beer or wine. There are commercial meat mixers available that make this job quite easy. Put the coarse ground meat in the mixer, pour in the seasonings, and mix for 10-15 minutes. Empty the seasoned meat into a bowl or tub and let it rest for an hour or so under refrigeration. If you don't have a meat mixer, I recommend mixing in a large rectangular plastic tub or dishpan. Start by leveling the meat to a uniform thickness. Then with your fingers extended, poke holes in the ground meat. (Visualize, if you will, aerating a lawn with a roller that has protruding metal spikes.) Then pour your dissolved seasonings over the surface with the holes and mix by hand for five to ten minutes. As with the meat mixer, let the meat rest under refrigeration for an hour or so before continuing to the next step.

Prior to re-grinding through a fine plate for the finished product, I like to re-mix the meat one more time just to insure an even distribution of the seasonings. If you're making bulk sausage, just re-grind and package. We prefer to use a vacuum packaging system and package bulk sausage or burger in 1 to 2 pound packages. If making link sausage when using this method, I install the stuffing tube and grind and stuff in one operation. Sausage stuffers are available, but I prefer to stuff my links as I grind and save the extra step. Refer to "Sausage Stuffing Tips" if you're making link sausage.

Cee Dub demonstrating how to stuff sausage into hog casings at Ranch Clinic 2008

Fant Steele Photo

Sweet Italian Sausage

Ingredients:

25 lb. meat (pork, beef, venison, or combination), cut into 1 1/2" cubes or strips, and chilled
16 Tbsp. fennel seed
3 Tbsp. salt
7 tsp. pepper
2 Tbsp. garlic powder
3 Tbsp. anise
8 Tbsp. sugar
9 Tbsp. Italian seasoning
3 Tbsp. fresh rosemary, finely chopped
4 Tbsp. basil
1 cup paprika
3 cups red wine

Place meat in a large tub. Thoroughly mix all the other ingredients in a bowl. Can let seasonings meld for at least an hour, stirring occasionally. Pour seasoning mixture over cold meat in tub and mix until meat is coated. Place in refrigerator for a minimum of 3 to 4 hours; overnight is better. Occasionally mix and turn seasoned meat to distribute seasoning throughout. Run the meat through a grinder into a separate container or links. Package into bags, label, and freeze.

Fant and Bill twisting stuffed sausage into links at Ranch Clinic 2008

Don Elliott Photo

Hot Italian Sausage

Ingredients:

25 lb. meat (pork, beef, venison, or combination),
    cut into 1 1/2" cubes or strips, and chilled
16 Tbsp. fennel seed
4 Tbsp. salt
8 tsp. pepper
2 Tbsp. garlic powder
2 Tbsp. anise
6 Tbsp. sugar
3 Tbsp. cayenne pepper
3 Tbsp. red pepper flakes
10 Tbsp. Italian seasoning
3 Tbsp. fresh rosemary, finely chopped
4 Tbsp. basil
1 cup paprika
3 cups red wine

Place meat in a large tub. Thoroughly mix all the other ingredients in a bowl. Can let seasonings meld for at least an hour, stirring occasionally. Pour seasoning mixture over cold meat in tub and mix until meat is coated. Place in refrigerator for a minimum of 3 to 4 hours; overnight is better. Occasionally mix and turn seasoned meat to distribute seasoning throughout. Run the meat through a grinder into a separate container or links. Package into bags, label, and freeze.

CEE DUB'S QUICK SAUSAGE

When Pen and I first contemplated introducing sausage making to our cooking demonstrations, we knew we had to streamline the process in order to keep the audience interested and be able to come up with a finished product in an hour or less. Trust me, it gets kind of boring watching someone grind meat, mix seasonings, then re-grind the same meat. Here is the method we developed to shorten the process from the "traditional method" of making sausage.

We start by cutting our grinding meat up into fairly small pieces. We prefer 1 inch cubes just like stew meat. Once the meat is cut, up we mix our seasonings and add them just as if the meat were already coarse ground. For demonstration purposes, we have the meat cut up ahead of time and chilled. We add the seasons and mix them in in front of the audience.

Taking the extra time to cut the grinding meat into small pieces increases the surface area the seasonings have access to and aids in an even distribution of the seasonings when we grind it. What we've found works best is to use a medium grinding plate on our grinder in lieu of first using a coarse plate followed by the fine plate.

When doing demonstrations we can grind, stuff links, and grill the finished product in less than an hour. At home, when using this method, we allow the links and/or bulk sausage to rest in the refrigerator overnight prior to packaging to allow the seasonings more time to blend with the ground meat.

Regardless of which method you choose, the end result will be better tasting and healthier than any store-bought sausage.

SAUSAGE SEASONINGS

For several years we utilized commercial seasoning mixes for all our sausage making. That's not to say we didn't play around with the taste factor a little bit. We like a bit more licorice flavor in our Italian sausage, so we would add more fennel seed to give us the flavor we wanted. Also we could spice up either breakfast or Italian sausage seasoning mixes by adding either cayenne pepper or dried red pepper flakes. On a German sausage mix that called for the addition of water, we added a good dark German beer for a slightly different flavor.

For the beginning sausage maker, there are lots of commercially available seasoning mixes that take a lot of the muss and fuss out of sausage making. But, you're still at the mercy of the company who packages them. If you use them, be a careful consumer and read the label. Many will have various preservatives, nitrites, and/or monosodium glutamate (MSG). If you plan to smoke your sausage, look for recipes that do include nitrites as they act as a preservative. Our recipes are for fresh sausage for immediate consumption and freezing.

Not being totally content with store-bought sausage seasonings, we began searching the internet for recipes, and then altering them to fit our personal tastes. We've found we can cut the salt by fifty to sixty percent and end up with sausage that tastes better to us and is obviously healthier. In addition we can add fresh herbs when available which gives a more robust flavor.

Words of Wisdom

Here's a simple, easy, no fuss method of rendering your own lard. Cut pork fat into 1/2" cubes and make a 1" deep layer of the cubes in a 9x9 inch glass or ceramic casserole dish. Microwave for 5 to 8 minutes. Pour off lard into a clean storage container.

TIPS FOR GRINDING MEAT

Trim meat well and cut into fairly uniform-size pieces. We find that cutting meat into strips results in a smoother flow into the auger .The size of the feed throat on your grinder will determine what size of chunks and strips you should use. Smaller pieces feed better. Try to avoid having to force large chunks into the grinder.

If using venison or other wild game, remove as much connective tissue as possible, trim out any bloodshot areas, and remove any stray hairs.

Clean and sterilize knives, cutting boards, grinders, grinder plates, blades, before starting. Make sure everyone working on the project wash hands frequently. Wear food service gloves if you prefer. A new toilet brush works well to clean the body of the grinder.

The colder the meat, the easier it will grind. If possible, set the containers of meat ready for grinding into the freezer for a couple of hours. If meat gets too warm, try sprinkling in a few ice chips as you grind.

Feed meat into the grinder at a uniform rate. Don't overload the grinder. Try to keep the auger at its fastest speed.

Keep all safety shields in place and DO NOT PUT YOUR FINGERS INTO THE GRINDER FOR ANY REASON UNLESS THE POWER CORD IS UNPLUGGED!

Grind meat into a clean tub or bowl; not the container it was in prior to grinding. Wash and disinfect bowls and tubs prior to any re-use.

If grinding large amounts of meat, work in small batches and keep everything not being processed under refrigeration.

Use good food scales to accurately weigh your meat. This will help with consistency between batches.

Keep a set of postal scales handy as well. They take the guess work out of dividing a large packet of commercial seasonings. Also, they are important if you're blending your own seasonings.

Before storing your grinder, wipe the cutting plate, blade, auger, and the inside body of the grinder with a THIN film of vegetable oil as a rust preventative.

Cee Dub using strips for grinding meat 2008

Welch Photo

═══ TIPS FOR STUFFING SAUSAGE ═══

When stuffing sausages, rinse and prepare the casings according to the package directions.

Moisten the stuffing tube before slipping the casing over the tube.

Get as long a casing as possible on the tube.

Start the grinder and slowly feed in meat until the stuffing tube is full. Shut off the grinder and tie a knot in the end of the casing.

Re-start the grinder and begin stuffing the casing. Use your thumb and forefinger to provide tension on the casing as it pulls off the stuffing tube. Do not fill casing too tight, it will rupture. You should be able to pinch the filled casing closed between your thumb and forefinger.

Stuff the entire casing full. Do not attempt to twist each link as it comes off the stuffing tube. Switching the grinder off and on to twist links will result in the electric motor overheating.

When the casing is nearly full, turn off the grinder, slip the remaining end of the casing off the stuffing tube, and tie it off with butcher string or an overhand knot.

Keep a bowl of warm water near the grinder. During the stuffing process keep dipping your fingers in the bowl of water and keep the casing moist.

To twist your links, lay the stuffed casing out on a large clean and sanitized work surface. With thumb and forefinger, gently pinch the casing for the desired length of link you want. Then with the other hand begin twisting the link away from your body. Twist it at least 6 to 8 times. Shift along the link and again pinch it with your thumb and forefinger. Twist the second link in the opposite direction of the first link. Continue twisting links in opposite directions until you reach the end of the casing. The opposite twists keep the links from unraveling.

Snip each link off the chain with kitchen shears and package.

Fant keeping the casing moist while stuffing the casing   Don Elliott Photo

11/15/2008 19:34

Fish & Fowl

Chicken Chile Rellanos

Ingredients:

½ lb. chicken breasts
1 Tbsp. chili powder
2 tsp. cumin
4 7 oz. cans whole green chiles, drained
1 lb. cheddar or longhorn cheese, grated
1 lb. Monterey Jack cheese, grated
5 eggs
4-5 Tbsp. flour
8-10 oz. evaporated milk, cream, or half and half
8-12 oz. green enchilada or taco sauce
1 lb. sour cream
Fresh cilantro, chopped

Cut chicken breasts across the grain into one inch chunks and put in pan with water to cover. Add chili powder and cumin. Simmer until done, or longer. Let cool in broth. Shred chicken by mashing with fingers. Return shredded chicken to broth and set aside until needed. Split the drained chiles so they will lay flat. Layer about half the chiles on the bottom of a 10" deep Dutch oven. Spread one half the cheeses over the chiles. Drain the shredded chicken and place on top of the cheese. Repeat layers of remaining chiles and cheese. Mix the eggs, flour, and milk or cream; pour over top. Cover and bake for about 45 minutes at around 350 degrees using 5-6 briquets under the DO and 12-14 briquets on the lid. If desired, drizzle some of the enchilada or taco sauce on top during the last 10 to 15 minutes of cooking. Let it set up for about 10 to 15 minutes before serving. Serve with sour cream, fresh cilantro, and remaining sauce.

Loren said that the guides and hunters at hunting camp demolish this in short order when they come dragging into camp a few hours after dark...and it holds well!

Loren Anderson
Salmon, Idaho

157

Coconut Shrimp and
Dipping Sauce

Ingredients

1 14 oz. can lite coconut milk, divided
1 ½ lbs. uncooked medium shrimp
1 jalapeno pepper, seeded and chopped
¼ cup minced fresh cilantro
¾ cup flour
4 egg whites
¾ cup panko
¾ cup flaked coconut,
    lightly toasted
1/3 cup apricot preserves
1 tsp. spicy brown mustard

Place 2 tablespoons coconut milk in a small bowl; cover and refrigerate.Peel and devein shrimp, leaving tails on. In a resealable plastic bag, combine the remaining coconut milk, jalapeno pepper, and cilantro. Add the shrimp to the bag and seal. Turn the bag to coat and refrigerate for 1 hour. Place flour in a small bowl. Lightly beat egg whites in another bowl. In a third bowl, combine panko and coconut. Remove shrimp from marinade; discard marinade. Dip shrimp in flour, then egg whites, then panko and coconut mixture. Place on a baking sheet coated with cooking spray. Bake at 400 degrees for about 8 minutes on each side, or until lightly browned. For dipping sauce, mix together reserved coconut milk, preserves, and mustard. Serves 3 to 4 as a main entrée, or about 5 as an appetizer.

NOTE: Rather than baking in an oven, place shrimp on an aluminum pizza pan that has been coated with cooking spray. Place pizza pan in a 14" or 16" Dutch oven and cover. Bake, using 14-16 briquets under the DO and 28-32 briquets on the lid. Bake for 7-9 minutes, until lightly brown; turn the shrimp and bake until brown.

Dutch Oven Fried Fish

Ingredients:

Fish filets
Cornmeal
Fish Fry™
Salt, pepper, lemon pepper, parsley, garlic
powder, etc., to taste
Non-stick spray

In a large ziploc bag, add a generous amount of corn meal, Fish Fry™, and whatever seasonings you chose; using a generous amount of the seasoning. Shake cornmeal and seasonings to mix well. Spray fish filets with non-stick spray; set aside. Cover bottom of Dutch oven with foil and spray with non-stick spray, covering well. Place fish in bag of seasoned cornmeal and shake fish to coat. Place filets in prepared Dutch oven. Spray again. Cover and bake at high heat, about 500 degrees, until brown; approximately 12 to 15 minutes on first side, and 15 minutes on second side.

Marshall Hawkes
Beaumont, Texas

Randy Riney, center, and friends getting some well-deserved R & R at LPR 2007   Welch Photo Collection

—————— Easy Baked Fish ——————

Ingredients:

4 tilapia fillets, or any white fish, about 4 oz. each
2 tsp. butter
¼ tsp. Old Bay™ seasoning, or to taste
½ tsp. garlic salt, or to taste
1 lemon, sliced
1 16 oz. package frozen mixed vegetables
Salt and pepper, to taste

Preheat a lightly greased 12" Dutch oven. Place the fish fillets in the bottom of the baking dish and dot with butter. Season with Old Bay seasoning and garlic salt. Top each one with a slice or two of lemon. Arrange the frozen mixed vegetables around the fish, and season lightly with salt and pepper. Bake for 25 to 30 minutes in the preheated oven, until vegetables are tender and fish flakes easily with a fork, using 7-9 briquets under the DO and about 20 briquets on the lid. Serves 2 to 4, depending on how hungry you are.

Marshall Hawkes
Beaumont, Texas

Wyatt looks like he doesn't quite believe the story Grandpa is reading to him
May 2007

Welch Photo Collection

—— Baked Chicken Parmesan ——

Ingredients:

4 boneless, skinless chicken breasts
1 egg, slightly beaten
¾ cup Italian seasoned bread crumbs
1 26 oz. favorite spaghetti sauce
1 cup shredded mozzarella cheese

Preheat oven or 12" Dutch oven lid to 400 degrees using 20-24 briquets. Spray 13 x 9 inch baking dish or DO with cooking spray. Dip chicken in egg, then bread crumbs, coating well. Arrange chicken pieces in baking vessel. Bake uncovered in oven or covered in Dutch oven for 20 to 30 minutes. Pour sauce over breasts and sprinkle cheese over pieces. Bake for additional 10 minutes or until chicken is no longer pink and thoroughly cooked. Serve with hot pasta or rice. Serves 4.

—— Five Can Casserole ——

Ingredients:

1 can boned whole chicken *
1 can cream of chicken soup
1 can cream of mushroom soup
1 can evaporated milk
1 can Chinese noodles
Grated cheddar cheese, if desired

Stir canned ingredients together and bake in a 12" Dutch oven for 25 minutes at 350 degrees, using 6-8 briquets under the DO and 20-22 briquets on the lid. Sprinkle the grated cheese on top and bake for another 10 minutes to melt cheese.

* If unable to find a whole boned chicken in a can, use 5 of the small cans of white meat and dark meat mixed.

Mike McLain
Montrose, Colorado

Fant's Minne-Mex Chicken and Wild Rice Casserole

When Fant Steele and his wife moved to Texas in 1980, they discovered Tex-Mex food, flavorful dishes such as enchiladas and fajitas. Many years later, upon moving to Minnesota, they encountered a more bland cuisine. In his travels these days, Fant finds DOG's (Dutch oven Gatherings) that are occurring in the local areas where he is traveling and working. Wanting to make a good impression at a DOG in Western Louisiana, he decided to prepare a Dutch oven dish with something famous from Minnesota, such as wild rice; but wanted to add a little Texas kick to chicken and wild rice. The following recipe is the result.

Ingredients:

2 Tbsp. extra virgin olive oil
1 lb. boneless, skinless chicken breasts,
    cut into 1" cubes
1/2 lb. onions, diced
1 1/3 cups diced celery
1 1/3 cups diced bell pepper, red, green, or yellow
1 8 oz. pkg. sliced mushrooms, chopped
2 Tbsp. minced garlic
1/2 lb. wild rice
3 cups chicken stock
1 10 oz. can Rotel Diced Tomatoes and Green
    Chilies™ mild, original, or hot
Lemon pepper and salt, to taste

All the vegetables should be diced into cubes about 1/4 inch in size. This can be done ahead of time and carried to camp in zip-top bags to reduce the preparation time when actually cooking. Wash the wild rice thoroughly before cooking by placing into a strainer and placing it under running water until the water runs clear. Follow the directions on the package to cook the rice.* Set rice aside.

Heat a 12" Dutch oven using 24 briquets under the oven. Add the olive oil and allow the oil to come to cooking temperature. Add the cubes of chicken to the pot and cook uncovered for 15 minutes, stirring occasionally. As the chicken cooks, use a spoon to break the chicken into smaller pieces until the chicken is about the consistency of pulled pork. Add the onions, celery, bell pepper, mushrooms, and garlic to the pot and stir. Season with lemon pepper and salt. Reduce the bottom heat to 9 briquets and place 15 of the briquets on the lid to bring the Dutch oven to 350 degrees. Cook for 15 minutes with the lid on. Add the wild rice, 2 cups of chicken stock, and Rotel™ to the pot. Reserve 1 cup of chicken stock. Cook for 1 1/2 hours with the lid on. Check the contents every 30 minutes. Add additional chicken stock if needed to allow the rice to cook without drying out. Serves 8.

* The more rice is washed before cooking, the milder the flavor.
* For firmer, nutty texture, decrease cooking time five to ten minutes.
* For fluffier, tender rice, increase cooking time five to ten minutes.
* Wild Rice should be cooked until it puffs, or blossoms, and the inside, lighter portion of the grain can be seen. Overcooking may cause mushiness.

Fant Steele
Rochester, Minnesota

163

Cee Dub demonstrating some sourdough techniques at Round Top, TX Clinic 2005   Welch Photo Collection

Marinated Shrimp

Ingredients:

2 lbs. cooked medium shrimp,
    peeled and deveined
1 medium purple onion, cut into rings
2 medium lemons, cut into slices
1 cup pitted ripe olives
½ cup olive oil
1/3 cup minced fresh parsley
3 Tbsp. red wine vinegar
3 Tbsp. lemon juice
1 clove garlic, minced
1 bay leaf
1 Tbsp. minced fresh basil, or
    1 tsp. dried basil
1 tsp. ground mustard
1 tsp. salt
¼ tsp. pepper

In a large serving bowl, combine the shrimp, onion rings, lemons and olives. In a jar with a tight-fitting led, combine the remaining ingredients and shake well. Pour over shrimp mixture and stir gently to coat. Cover and refrigerate for 24 hours, stirring occasionally. Remove bay leaf before serving. Serves 12 to 14.

Hampton's Lemon Chicken and Rice

Ingredients:

1 large ripe lemon
1 lb. boneless skinless
    chicken breasts
1 tsp. paprika
1 tsp. black pepper
2 tsp. olive oil
1 tsp. oregano
1 14 oz. can chicken broth, plus
    1 can water
1 cup uncooked rice, brown or white or wild
¼ cup parsley, finely chopped

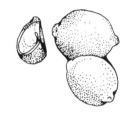

Grate rind off lemon; set aside. Cut chicken breasts into bite size pieces; sprinkle with paprika and pepper. Sauté seasoned chicken pieces in hot olive oil until no longer pink. Add grated lemon rind, juice from lemon, and oregano. Add chicken broth and water; add rice and bring to a boil. Cover and let simmer 30-35 minutes. Add parsley; mix well and serve. Serves 6. NOTES: A variation is to add one package frozen mixed vegetables. Also, can substitute bottled lemon juice to taste for fresh lemon and rind.

Kirby and Carol Hampton
Bonners Ferry, Idaho

Words of Wisdom

Most Store-bought herbs and spices are expensive. The small 0.9 ounce bottles often cost $3.00 or more. Check out the cellophane-wrapped spices in the Hispanic section. Often one can buy oregano, chili powder, basil, cinnamon, bay leaves, etc., for less than a dollar.

Mogollon Rim Chicken with ────Southwestern Rice────

Ingredients:

1 chicken, cut into serving pieces, or
    about 8 pieces of legs, thighs, and breasts
1 cup flour
Salt and pepper to taste
1/3 stick butter or margarine
1 bunch green onions, chopped
1 green bell pepper, chopped
1 small jar pimientos, chopped
2 cloves garlic, diced
2 cups white rice, uncooked
½ tsp. chili powder
2 tsp. comino
4 cups chicken broth

Preheat the lid of a 12" Dutch oven using 20-22 briquets for 15-20 minutes. Dredge chicken pieces in salted and peppered flour. Brown in butter melted in DO. Remove chicken from DO onto plate. In the drippings sauté green onions, green pepper, pimiento peppers, and garlic about 1 minute. Add rice and stir in with vegetables about 1 minute. Add chili powder, comino, salt and pepper to taste. Lay the chicken pieces on top. Add the chicken broth. Put the lid on the DO and cook for about 45 minutes using 6-8 briquets under the DO, or at 350 degrees in the oven, until the liquid cooks away and the rice is done. Serves 4 to 6. Serve with Spinach and Pineapple Salad.

Sherry and Delmar Hiller
Carolyn and Danny Wheat
Hunt, Texas

Rosie begging for a little sample from Sherry at the Hunt Clinic November 2006   Truitt Photo Collection

---

—— Poached Dill Mustard Salmon ——

Ingredients:

1 salmon fillet
Dill mustard
1/3 cup peach chardonnay or white wine
Aluminum foil

Spread out double layers of aluminum foil allowing for generous folding to close foil on top and ends; making a packet. Lay salmon fillet on foil. Spread dill mustard generously on fillet, and add wine. Fold foil on top, and fold or twist ends so the fish will poach in the wine. Cook on BBQ or in oven for about 30 minutes, or until done. Serve as a main dish or as a component to Dill Salmon Chowder*.

Hobart Manns
Portland, Oregon

* Dill Salmon Chowder recipe is found in "Soups, Stews, & Chilis" section

—————— Shrimp Scampi ——————

Ingredients:

1 ½ lb. shrimp, peeled and deveined
¾ stick butter or margarine
4 cloves garlic, minced
1 large egg, well beaten
¼ cup white wine
1 tsp. Worcestershire sauce
2 green onions, chopped
Salt and pepper to taste

In a large skillet or 12" Dutch oven, heat butter or margarine; add garlic and sauté. Dip the shrimp in the beaten egg and place them in the hot skillet. Sauté shrimp about three minutes. Reduce heat and add the white wine, Worcestershire sauce, green onions, and seasonings; heat through. Serve over a bed of hot rice. Serves 4 to 6.

Cee Dub and Pen's Christmas camp for a late elk hunt on the bank of the Salmon River above Riggins, Idaho. Santa even found the stockings there!   Welch Photo Collection

Seafood Delight

Ingredients:

1-2 Tbsp. butter or margarine
2-3 lbs. salmon fillet
1 can cream of mushroom soup
10 oz. sour cream
1/3 cup chopped onion
1 tsp. fish seasoning
¾ cup crab meat, or,
    Imitation crab
¾ cup bay shrimp
¾ cup grated cheddar cheese
¾ tsp. dill weed

Lay out a double thickness of aluminum foil large enough to completely wrap salmon fillet in for cooking. Smear butter or margarine on the middle, and lay salmon fillet on the butter or margarine. Mix together mushroom soup and sour cream, equal parts, onions, and fish seasoning. Smear mixture on fillet. Sprinkle crab meat and shrimp over the top. Sprinkle the cheese over the seafood. Sprinkle dill weed on top. Roll up fillet completely. Bake at 350 degrees for about 45 minutes in the oven, BBQ grill, or 12" Dutch oven, using 6-8 briquets under the oven and 18-22 briquets on the lid.

Herb Good
Hood River, Oregon

Words of Wisdom

When rafting or horse packing, crack your eggs ahead of time, putting them in a plastic storage jar with a screw-on lid. If you flip a boat or roll a pack horse, you at least don't have broken eggs to clean up. Make sure to keep your eggs as cold as possible.

Ranch Turkey

Ranch guests, Callum and Kimi Cook spent Thanksgiving 2007 with us here at Las Piedras Ranch. Dinner was a collaborative effort with them preparing the turkey for me to cook in a 15" MACA Dutch oven. Not only was their preparation different than anything I'd seen previously, but they also passed on a different roasting technique that makes perfect sense.

Ingredients:

1 12-14 lb. turkey
Black pepper
Salt
Sage
Dried thyme
2 lemons, sliced
2 oranges, sliced
3 medium onions, sliced, divided
Fresh rosemary
Fresh thyme
1 lb. carrots

Twenty-four hours before cooking, remove giblets and rinse turkey with cold water. Dust the body cavity with black pepper, salt, sage and thyme. Slice the oranges, lemons, and one onion. Place slices of lemon, orange, and one onion in the body cavity. Next, separate the skin from the meat and insert sprigs of fresh rosemary and thyme on the breast. Sprinkle outside with coarse black pepper and refrigerate until time to cook. Prior to roasting, place a layer of onions and carrots on the bottom of the Dutch oven and place turkey in oven breast side down. While roasting, the liquid cooking out in the body from the citrus and onion slices in the cavity will seep downward into the breast meat adding extra flavor. Arrange remaining carrot and onion slices around the bird. Roast for about 2 hours with 24-30 briquets on top and 10-12 on the bottom, changing coals as needed. Then, reach into the

Dutch oven with two meat forks and carefully lift and turn turkey breast side up. Add fresh briquets to the lid to finish roasting and brown the breast. NOTE: When cooking this in your home oven, liberally butter the bird and place strips of bacon over the bird while roasting.

Turkeys in the back yard at Cee Dub and Pen's house in Grangeville, ID

Welch Photo Collection

Shrimp Pie

Ingredients:

½ stick butter or margarine
1 lb. shrimp, deveined and peeled
1 medium onion, chopped
2 ribs celery, chopped
½ green pepper, chopped
4 cloves garlic, minced
Salt and pepper, to taste
¼ tsp. cayenne pepper
Cajun seasoning, to taste
1 10 oz. can cream of mushroom soup
2 unbaked pie shells

In a skillet, sauté shrimp in butter or margarine for five minutes, remove, and set aside. Add onion, celery, green pepper, garlic, and sauté for ten minutes. Season shrimp and add to the vegetables along with the soup; and, cook 15 minutes. If too thick, add a little white wine, oyster liquor, water, or chicken broth. Place in pie shell and cover with other pie shell. Cut slits in top shell to allow steam to escape. Bake at 350 degrees until lightly browned and done.

—— Spicy Tuscan Chicken ** ——

Ingredients:

3 Tbsp. olive oil
3 boneless, skinless chicken breasts,
    cut into bite-size pieces
2 cloves garlic, minced
1 15 oz. can cannellini or white beans, drained
1 15 oz. can kidney beans, drained
3 cups loosely packed fresh spinach leaves
3 Tbsp. lemon juice
1 ½ tsp. dried crushed rosemary, or,
    1 tsp. finely chopped fresh rosemary
¾ tsp. red pepper flakes
½ tsp. salt
½ cup white wine, chicken broth, or water

Heat oil in skillet saucepan. Add chicken pieces and brown, cooking thoroughly. Lower heat and add remaining ingredients. Cover and simmer 10 minutes. Serve with rice. Serves 4 to 6.

** A photo of this recipe is featured at the beginning of the "Fish and Fowl" section.

Cee Dub going for a ride in Clevengers' sleigh across the river from the house in Grangeville 2004

Welch Photo Collection

Ann's Easy Enchiladas

Ingredients:

1 lb. chicken tenders
1 can cream of chicken soup
½ can evaporated milk
1 4 oz. can green chilis
1 lb. Monterey Jack cheese, grated, divided
10 flour tortillas

Boil chicken until nearly done and starting to separate. Drain, cool, shred, and set aside. In a saucepan, heat up soup, milk, and chilis. Load a portion of chicken, then shredded cheese flour tortillas, using about one half the cheese. Roll each tortilla up and place in 13 x 9 inch baking dish or 12" Dutch oven. Pour soup mixture over the enchiladas. Put remaining cheese on top. Bake at 350 degrees for 30 minutes. If using DO, cover, and bake for 30 minutes using 6-8 briquets under the DO and 18-22 on the lid. Makes 10 enchiladas.

Ann Dykas
Eagle, Idaho

Abigail enjoying some boogie boarding in McCall, Idaho 2008

Dykas Photo Collection

Tarragon Chicken

Ingredients:

3 cups uncooked egg noodles
1 lb. boneless skinless chicken breasts.
¾ tsp. dried tarragon
¾ tsp. lemon-pepper seasoning
1 Tbsp. butter
2 cups sliced fresh mushrooms
4 garlic cloves, minced
2 cups chicken broth, divided
3 Tbsp. flour
¼ cup sour cream

Cook noodles according to directions; drain and set aside. Sprinkle chicken breasts with tarragon and lemon-pepper. In a large nonstick or cast iron skillet, over medium heat, brown chicken in butter on both sides. Remove breasts from skillet and keep warm. Add mushrooms and garlic to skillet drippings and sauté until tender. Add one cup broth, stirring to loosen the browned bits from pan. Return chicken to pan and bring to a boil. Reduce heat, simmer uncovered, until chicken juices run clear. Remove chicken and keep warm. Combine flour and remaining broth until smooth and stir into pan juices. Bring to a boil, stir, and cook for 2 minutes or until thickened. Remove from heat, stir in sour cream. Serve chicken on noodles and top with sauce.

Words of Wisdom

To improve the taste of meats dredged in flour before frying, season the meat first rather than using seasoned flour. You will use much less seasoning and the seasoning will be on the meat rather than the breading. The same rule applies to fish being battered before frying.

Vernon Hayes Photo

Meats

Baked Linguine with
Meat Sauce

Ingredients:

3 Tbsp. olive oil
2 lbs. ground venison or beef
2 cloves garlic, minced
2 14 oz. cans diced tomatoes
6 oz. tomato sauce
1 tsp. salt
2 tsp. sugar
8 oz. linguine
16 oz. sour cream
8 oz. cream cheese, softened
1 bunch green onions, chopped
8 oz. cheddar cheese, grated

In a large skillet, heat oil. Add meat and garlic and cook until browned. Stir in tomatoes, tomato sauce, tomato paste, salt and sugar. Simmer for 30 minutes and set aside. Cook pasta according to package directions. Drain and place in lightly oiled casserole dish or 12" Dutch oven. In bowl, stir together sour cream, cream cheese, and onions. Spread over pasta and top with meat sauce. Bake at 350 degrees for 20 to 25 minutes or until bubbly. If baking in a DO, cover and bake using 6-8 briquets under the DO and 18-22 briquets on the lid. Sprinkle on cheese, continue to bake until cheese melts.

Words of Wisdom

When freezing fresh blackberries, first let them freeze for about an hour on cookie sheets before packaging in bags with a vacuum sealer. When thawed, they will still be individual berries instead of a gooey glob of blackberries. Also do the same thing after blanching asparagus before packaging.

Beef and Carrot Stir Fry

Ingredients:

1 ½ lbs. beef, thinly sliced into 3" strips
Salt and pepper, to taste
3 Tbsp. vegetable or olive oil, divided
3 cloves garlic, sliced thin or minced
¾ cup baby carrots, cut into ¾" pieces
2 Tbsp. cornstarch
¾ cup beef broth
2 Tbsp. soy sauce
2 tsp. grated orange peel
1 tsp. ground ginger

Season meat and set aside. In a large skillet or wok, heat 2 tablespoons oil. Add garlic and sauté until done. Remove and set aside. Fry beef in batches until meat reaches desired doneness; remove, and keep warm. Add remaining oil. Stir fry carrots for 5 minutes. In a bowl, mix cornstarch and broth until smooth. Add the soy sauce, orange peel, and ginger. Return garlic and beef to skillet or wok with carrots. Stir in broth mixture. Bring to a boil and cook for 2 minutes, stirring constantly, until thickened. Serve over rice. Serves 4.

Cee Dub and Scooter doing ranch chores in Dynamite, the old ranch truck, Summer 2008   Welch Photo Collection

Cajun Rib Casserole

Ingredients:

5 lbs. rib ends or small pork chops
1½ cups flour
¼ cup Cajun seasoning
Oil for frying
2 cups rice, uncooked
4 cups water
1 Tbsp. hot pepper sauce
2 tsp. Worcestershire sauce
½ green pepper, sliced
½ large onion, sliced
1 28 oz. can stewed tomatoes
Salt and pepper, to taste

Coat ribs with Cajun seasoning. Dredge them in flour. Fry in very hot oil until brown. Remove from oil and drain. Place ribs in deep 12" or 14" Dutch oven or ovenproof pan. Sprinkle rice on top. Add water, sauces, green bell pepper, onion, tomatoes, and seasonings. Cover DO or pan with foil and bake at 350 degrees for an hour using 8-10 briquets underneath and 18-22 briquets on the lid.

Cee Dub cutting up the wild pig ribs, homemade sausage, and brisket for dinner at the Ranch Clinic 2008

Fant Steele Photo

178

Cheeseburger Buns

Ingredients:

2 envelopes active dry yeast, ¼ oz. each
½ cup warm water, 110 to 115 degrees
¾ cup warm milk, 110 to 115 degrees
¼ cup sugar
¼ cup shortening
1 egg
1 tsp. salt
3 1/2-4 cups all-purpose flour
1 ½ lbs. ground beef
¼ cup chopped onion
1 8 oz. can tomato sauce
8 slices American cheese, halved
Hamburger dill pickles, optional

In a mixing bowl, dissolve yeast in warm water. Add milk, sugar, shortening, egg, salt, and 2 cups flour; beat until smooth. Stir in enough flour to form a soft dough. Turn onto a floured surface; knead until smooth and elastic, about 4 to 6 minutes. Place in a greased bowl, turning once to grease top. Cover and let rise in a warm place until doubled in size, about 30 minutes. In a skillet, cook beef and onion until meat is no longer pink; drain. Stir in tomato sauce. Remove from heat; set aside to cool. Punch dough down; divide into 16 pieces. On a lightly floured surface, gently roll our and stretch each piece into a 5-inch circle. Top each circle with a piece of cheese, about 3 tablespoons of the beef mixture, and 2 to 3 dill pickle slices, if desired. Bring dough over filling to the center; pinch edges together to seal. Place seam-side down on a greased baking sheet. Cover and let rise in a warm place until doubled, about 20 minutes. Bake at 400 degrees for 8 to 12 minutes or until golden brown. Serve immediately. Refrigerate leftovers. Makes 16 sandwiches.

Chalene McGrath
Providence, Utah

Cornbread Meat Pie

Ingredients:

1 lb. ground meat
1 cup yellow cornmeal
2 eggs, well beaten
1 cup milk
½ tsp. baking soda
¾ tsp. salt
1 can cream-style corn
½ cup bacon drippings, shortening, or oil
1 large onion, chopped
½ lb. sharp cheddar cheese, grated
1 4 oz. can jalapeno peppers or green chiles, diced
2 Tbsp. cornmeal

Brown the ground meat, drain, and set aside. Mix together in a bowl the cup of cornmeal, eggs, milk, baking soda, salt, corn, and bacon drippings and set aside. Mix together in another bowl the onion and jalapenos. Sprinkle the remaining cornmeal in a 12" Dutch oven or a large cast iron skillet, brown slightly, and make a thin layer. Pour one-half the batter in the DO or skillet. Sprinkle evenly, one at a time, the cheese, meat, and onion and pepper mixture. Pour remaining batter on top. Cover the Dutch oven. Bake 45 to 50 minutes at 350 degrees. Place 5-7 briquets under the oven and 19-22 on the lid. Let the dish rest a few minutes after removing from heat to allow cheese to set up for easier slicing before serving. Serve with a green salad for a terrific meal. Serves 6 to 8.

Sandy Riney
Las Piedras Ranch
Real County, Texas

—— Easy Louisiana Style Gumbo ——

Ingredients:

½ stick butter

1/3 cup flour

2 Tbsp. vegetable or olive oil

1 lb. sausage (Kielbasa, mild or hot Italian, or
    Chorizo), cut into ½ inch slices

1 tsp. Cajun seasoning

3 cloves garlic, chopped

1 green pepper, cut into small pieces

1 medium onion, chopped

1 16 oz. can crushed tomatoes, undrained

2 cups chopped fresh okra, or
    1 10 oz. pkg. frozen okra, thawed and chopped

1 14 oz. can chicken broth

1 cup fresh or frozen green beans,
    cut into 1 ½ inch pieces

1 tsp. red pepper sauce

1 lb. frozen shrimp

1 box (4 pkg.) boil-in-a-bag rice per batch of Gumbo

Melt butter in saucepan or skillet. Heat butter and add flour, stirring constantly. Cook roux to desired darkness; set aside. In saucepan or 12" Dutch oven, heat oil and brown the sausage. Sprinkle on Cajun seasoning while cooking. Add garlic, green pepper, and onions. Sauté until slightly brown. Add tomatoes, okra, chicken broth, green beans, and red pepper sauce. Add shrimp to pan. Bring to a boil. Reduce heat and simmer 5 minutes, or until shrimp are hot and pink. Thicken with roux, adding in small amounts and stirring in until desired thickness is reached. Serve with hot cooked rice.

Penny Welch
Mountain Home, Texas

Pen's Lasagna

Ingredients:

1½ lbs. Italian sausage or hamburger
4 cloves garlic, minced (or garlic powder)
1 Tbsp. basil leaves
1 medium onion, chopped
½ tsp. salt
½ tsp. pepper
1 large can tomatoes, undrained, diced
2 small cans tomato paste
1 small can tomato sauce
¾ cup red wine optional
1 10 oz. pkg. lasagna noodles

Brown meat slowly in skillet; spoon off fat. Add garlic, basil, onion, salt, pepper, tomatoes, tomato sauce, tomato paste, and wine. Simmer, uncovered, about 30 minutes, stirring occasionally. Cook lasagna noodles until tender in boiling, salted water, about 15 minutes. Drain, rinse in cold water, and set aside.

Cheese Filling Ingredients:

4 cups ricotta cheese
½ cup Parmesan or Romano cheese
2 Tbsp. parsley flakes
2 eggs, beaten
2 tsp. salt
½ tsp. pepper
1 lb. mozzarella cheese, grated or thinly sliced

Mix all ingredients except mozzarella cheese. Place a very thin layer of sauce on the bottom of a 13 x 9 inch baking dish or a 12" Dutch oven, then one-half the noodles. Spread with one-half the cheese mixture. Cover with one-half the mozzarella cheese; then with one-half the meat mixture. Repeat layers. Bake at 375 degrees for 45 minutes. If using a DO, put the lid on. Bake using 6-8 briquets underneath and 20-22 briquets on the lid. Let stand 10 minutes after baking. Serves 10 to 12, but closer to 6 to 8 if you really like lasagna! NOTE: This recipe is large enough that it makes quite a big batch. Or, divide the ingredients and make a 13 x 9 inch, or 12" DO, batch; and a small batch in a loaf pan.

Penny Welch
Mountain Home, Texas

——— Fruit Glazed Pork Chops ———

Ingredients:

4 (¾" thick) pork chops (about 2 lbs.)
1 Tbsp. oil
6 oz. package diced fruit and raisin mix
¼ cup minced onion
1 cup orange-pineapple juice
½ tsp. salt
¼ tsp. dry mustard
¼ tsp. ground ginger
2 Tbsp. water
2 Tbsp. corn starch

In large cast iron skillet or 12" Dutch oven, brown pork chops in oil using medium to high heat. Drain off excess fat. Sprinkle fruit and onion over meat. Blend together juice, salt, mustard, and ginger; add to meat and fruit. Reduce heat, cover, and cook very slowly until pork is tender, about 40 minutes. Remove chops to serving dish. Thoroughly blend water and corn starch, and add to fruit and drippings in pan. Stir over medium heat until thickened. Pour sauce over meat. Serves 4.

Sandy Riney
Las Piedras Ranch
Real County, Texas

Pork Chops 'n' Stuffing

Loren told us how this recipe came to be. He said, "Way back some 30 odd years ago when I first came to the Salmon country, another character and I rattled into Peterson Lake west of Leadore for a few days of fishing. I had a new 10" DO and wasn't even sure which end to stuff the food in! At any rate, knowing a good pork chop is hard to beat, that I could make a meal of just stuffing, and that apples and pork were made for each other, I threw 'em all in the little Dutch – good! Still one of my favorites today...and, it's just TOO simple."

Ingredients:

3-4, ¾" pork chops
2 Tbsp. oil
1 box MJB™ wild rice stuffing; or,
     whatever flavor turns your crank
Herbs and spices, to taste
2-3 Granny Smith apples, sliced

Brown pork chops in oil in hot 10" Dutch oven. Remove and drain off excess oil. Mix stuffing as per box instructions and put in bottom of DO. Arrange chops over stuffing and sprinkle on desired herbs and spices. Cover with sliced apples and bake 45 minutes to an hour using 5-6 briquets under the DO and 12-14 briquets on the lid. For a drier stuffing, use less liquid than called for in cooking instructions since the apples and chops will add additional moisture.

Loren Anderson
Salmon, Idaho

Words of Wisdom

Scrub and wash vegetables such as potatoes, carrots, turnips, etc., instead of peeling them. You keep a lot more of the nutrients and you have less garbage to deal with.

Trina, Brian, and Matt in Moscow for Brian's graduation
from U of I May 2007   Welch Photo Collection

—— Pork Chops and Sauerkraut ——

After Trina gave us this recipe, it became a favorite at demos, not only delicious, but so easy!

Ingredients:

4 pork chops or steaks, whole or
    cut into 1 inch pieces
1 Tbsp. vegetable oil
3 cloves garlic, finely chopped
1 14 oz. can sauerkraut, with caraway seeds,
    if desired
3 Roma tomatoes, cubed
½ tsp. paprika

Brown chops or steaks on each side in hot oil in cast iron skillet or 10" Dutch oven. Add garlic and continue to sauté until cooked. Pour the sauerkraut over the pork and put tomatoes on top of sauerkraut. Sprinkle with paprika. Cover, reduce heat, and simmer at least 20 minutes, until pork chops are tender or by putting 5 briquets under the DO and 8-10 on the lid. NOTE: A variation we have used is to add a cup of chopped celery mixed with the tomatoes.

Trina Dykas
Boise, Idaho

Rich's Camp
———— Stew and Biscuits ————

Ingredients:

3 chicken breasts
3 Tbsp. oil
1 medium onion, chopped
2 cloves garlic, minced
6 medium potatoes, peeled and cut into quarters
lengthwise
3 cans cream of celery soup
Part of 1 beer

Cut chicken breasts into jojo style pieces, approximately 6 per whole breast. Heat oil in 12" Dutch oven and brown chicken pieces in hot oil. Remove chicken and sauté onion and garlic. Drain off any excess oil. Place chicken pieces back in DO with onion and garlic. Add potatoes to the oven. Stir soup and beer together and pour over top of other ingredients. Cook at 350 degrees for 1 to 1 1//2 hours, using 6-8 briquets under the DO and 18-22 on the lid. Change out charcoal after about an hour. Prepare Rich's Beer Biscuits, below, and put on top of the mixture when potatoes are nearly done. Cook for about 35 minutes longer or until biscuits are golden brown.

Rich's Beer Biscuits

Combine beer and Bisquick™ until it is thick enough to drop off a spoon onto a baking sheet. Bake at 350 degrees until golden brown.

Rich Wilson
Genesee, Idaho

186

Betty's Corned
────── Beef & Dumplings ──────

On my list of favorite childhood meals, this quick simple recipe is number two, right behind Mom's fried chicken dinner on Sunday afternoon. Mom made this in an electric skillet and I've adapted it to a Dutch oven. These many years later I marvel at how Mom could whip together such tasty and simple meals in just minutes. These days when I make this recipe, the memories from long ago come back when I open the cans of corned beef. It's the only can I know of that still opens by taking the key off the can and winding up the strip of soldered metal.

Ingredients:

2 cans corned beef
1 medium onion, diced
1 Tbsp. vegetable oil
1 ½ cups tomato juice

Dumplings:

2 cups flour
1 Tbsp. baking powder
Pinch of salt
1/3 cup vegetable oil
1 cup milk or buttermilk

Break the corned beef up and sauté for a few minutes along with the diced onion in a small amount of vegetable oil. Add the tomato juice and simmer. While the corned beef simmers, in a bowl mix the dry ingredients for the dumplings before adding the liquid ingredients. Use about 2 tablespoons of dough for each dumpling. Space the dumplings about an inch apart. Bake for 15-20 minutes with 6-8 briquets underneath and 18-22 on top. NOTES: For a spicy version of this recipe use a Spicy Bloody Mary mix instead of the tomato juice. You can also add ½ cup shredded sharp cheddar cheese to the dumplings.

Sourdough
—————— Chicken-Fried Steak ** ——————

Ingredients:

6-8 tenderized steaks, beef or pork
Salt and pepper, to taste
2-3 cups sourdough starter
1-2 cups vegetable oil
2 cups flour

Season both sides of the steaks. Pour the sourdough starter in a shallow bowl and set aside. Heat the oil in a Dutch oven or a deep skillet over medium to high heat to 375 degrees. While the oil heats, dredge the steaks in flour first, then into the sourdough starter, completely coating the steak. Dip the steaks into the flour again and then place into the hot oil, 2 or 3 at a time, so the oil does not lose too much heat. Cook the steaks until golden brown, turning once, about 4 to 6 minutes. Carefully place the steaks on paper towels to drain. Serve with gravy, steak sauce, or ketchup.

** A photo of this recipe is featured at the beginning of the "Meats" section.

Everyone reaping the fruits of their day's labor and chowing down at the Ranch Clinic May 2008
Fant Steele Photo

Roast Rack of Pork
——— with Sweet Potatoes ———

Ingredients:

4 Tbsp. olive oil, divided
1 Tbsp. orange zest
2 Tbsp. slivers of lemon peel
2 cloves garlic, sliced
Coarse black pepper
Four-bone rack of pork
           approximately 4 lbs
4 medium sweet potatoes
1 medium onion, sliced
½ cup white wine or chicken broth
Salt

Mix 2 tablespoons olive oil, orange zest, slivers of lemon peel, garlic, and coarse black pepper; and place in a gallon resealable bag. Place rack of pork in the bag and turn to coat meat. Allow to marinate for 2 to 3 hours, turning occasionally. Trim, rinse, and dry the sweet potatoes. When dry, wipe skins with a remaining olive oil. Place the onion slices in a 12" Dutch oven, covering the bottom. Place rack of pork in the Dutch oven and drizzle marinade over the top. Add white wine or chicken broth and slow roast with 12-14 briquets on top and 5-7 on the bottom, for an hour. Then place the whole sweet potatoes around the roast, replace the charcoal, and roast for another hour. If roasting in the oven, the roast can be browned in each side at a high temperature, then covered and roasted for one hour, then uncovered for another hour at 325 degrees.

——— Words of Wisdom ———

For camp biscuit cutters, use washed out cans. Then you can make biscuits of varying sizes.

DO NOT PEEK !

What do kids at Christmas time and beginning Dutch oven cooks have in common? It's been my first hand experience with both that they possess an almost overpowering urge to "peek"! In the case of kids, this behavior intensifies between the time the first package is placed under the Christmas tree until Christmas Day. On the other hand, beginning Dutch oven cooks, and in some cases cooks with a fair amount of experience, have that same overpowering urge to peek just minutes after they start a recipe cooking in their Dutch oven! Of course, in the child's case consequences result if they are caught. For the Dutch oven cook, the consequences occur the instant they take off the lid for a "peek" at what's cooking whether they get caught peeking or not!

Most of us remember getting our hands slapped, or some other portion of our anatomy slapped, when as children we opened mother's oven door to see if the baking cookies or cake were done yet. In my case, being a slow learner, it took many slaps to convince me to wait until they were "really done." These many years later it's very obvious why mothers must sometimes resort to corporal punishment for the "gross misdemeanor" of prematurely opening the oven door. With the oven door open, heat escapes. Of course a modern electric or gas oven is capable of quickly recovering that heat loss with the twist of a dial. However, repeatedly opening the door will increase the cooking time of whatever is being cooked.

When a Dutch oven cook lifts off the lid for a quick peek, the same loss of heat occurs. But, the Dutch oven cook does not have the capability to quickly recover that lost heat by twisting a dial. Using a Camp Chef Dutch oven with their patented thermometer aperture, we've tested for heat loss when someone takes a quick peek. With the oven at approximately 375 degrees, a peek of 2 seconds results in a loss of 50 degrees! In the case of baking biscuits, the drop in temperature has definite consequences. The biscuits will continue to bake, but the high temperature

190

that is needed to brown the biscuits has been lost. Of course the heat will slowly recover, but the total time necessary to bake the biscuits will be extended. Those are the consequences of just one peek. Additional peeks will seriously extend the cooking time.

For folks making the conversion from the home oven to the Dutch oven, the stumbling block is the fact that a Dutch oven does not have a glass top to peek through as does one's home oven. Not being able to see what's going on inside the Dutch oven is the unknown factor that can cause a serious case of "peekitis" to develop. Over the years I've had several clinic participants whom I threatened with handcuffs in order to get them to just leave well enough alone and let things cook without peeking.

So, if a person does have a case of "peekitis", how do we cure the affliction? The simple cures are confidence and trust! For the purpose of this discussion, let's assume we're cooking with moderate summertime temperatures and no wind factor to worry about. For any given recipe, one should follow the recipe for both the amount of heat and the approximate cooking time given as a rule of thumb. With an eye on the clock as the time given in the recipe approaches, the cook should begin to smell the recipe cooking. Our nose is a very sensitive instrument when it comes to telling our brain whether the grub in our Dutch oven is cooking, done, or burnt. This gives rise to what we call in our camp, the "Smell Test". If it smells done, it's done; if it smells burnt, it's burnt; and if you can't smell it, it ain't done! A former clinic student of ours from Ozona, Texas, Craig Deaton, puts it another way, "If you're lookin', it ain't cookin'!"

Though folks always laugh when I tell them about the smell test, most folks have experienced this same phenomenon in their home kitchens! How many times have any of us put something in the oven, not set the timer, and then got involved in some other activity around the house totally forgetting about what's in the oven. Our brain only hits the "refresh" button when we smell what's cookin', i.e., it's done, or it's burnt! So,...

My advice for anyone suffering from "peekitis" is to first keep an eye on their clock; and, secondly make sure they're downwind from their Dutch oven as the time given in their recipe approaches. Of course cooking times will always vary depending on weather conditions, but keeping the lid on and resisting that urge to peek, especially when baking, will pay dividends such as being able to serve on time and not having your guests leave!

Stuffed Eggplant

Ingredients:

2 small eggplants
3 Tbsp. vegetable or olive oil
½ lb. favorite bulk sausage
1 onion, chopped
1 tomato, chopped
3 cloves garlic, minced
3 Tbsp. olive oil
1 tsp. salt
½ tsp. pepper
½ tsp. oregano
¾ cup water
½ cup fresh parsley, chopped
¼ lb. cheddar cheese, grated

Wash eggplant and cut in half lengthwise. Remove pulp leaving about one-quarter inch pulp in shell. Dice up removed pulp. Heat oil in large skillet and sauté pulp, sausage, onions, tomatoes, garlic, salt, pepper, and oregano. When meat is thoroughly browned, add water and parsley. Simmer for five minutes. Stuff eggplant shells with sautéed mixture. Place in baking dish or 12" Dutch oven. Cover DO. Bake at 350 degrees for about 30 minutes using 6-8 briquets under DO and 18-22 briquets on the lid. Top with cheese and bake five minutes more until cheese is melted. Makes 4 servings.

—— Seasoned Beef Tenderloin ——

Ingredients:

1 tsp. dried oregano
1 tsp. paprika
1 tsp. dried thyme
½ tsp garlic powder
½ tsp. onion powder
½ tsp. pepper
½ tsp. white pepper
¼ tsp. cayenne pepper
½ cup brown mustard
3 lb. beef tenderloin

Combine dry seasonings. Brush brown mustard on tenderloin, coating entire surface area. Rub seasonings over entire tenderloin. Tenderloin can be wrapped tightly and refrigerated overnight for a more intense flavor. If refrigerated, bring to room temperature before cooking. Place seasoned tenderloin on a bed of sliced onions or a rack in a 12" deep Dutch oven. Bake at 425 degrees using 8-10 briquets under the oven and 22-24 briquets on the lid until meat is cooked as desired. For medium-rare, cook for about 45 minutes or until a meat thermometer reads 145 degrees; 65 minutes for medium and 160 degrees; and, 70 minutes for well-done and 170 degrees. If cooking in oven, bake uncovered. Let stand for 10 minutes before carving. Makes 8 to 10 servings.

Longhorn cattle drive through streets of Fort Worth, Texas

Welch Photo Collection

193

——— Venison Scallopine ———

Ingredients:

2 medium onions, sliced
3 cloves garlic, minced
¼ cup butter
2 lbs. thinly sliced venison steak, or
    thinly sliced beef round steak
8 oz. fresh mushrooms, sliced
¼ tsp. pepper
2 tsp. paprika
1/3 cup chopped fresh parsley
1 ½ cups beef bouillon
1 ½ cups sour cream
4 Tbsp. flour
1 16 oz. package wide noodles

In 12" Dutch oven, sauté onions and garlic in butter until soft. Add venison or beef and brown on all sides. Add mushrooms and continue to sauté. Add pepper, paprika, parsley, and bouillon; and stir well. Reduce heat and simmer covered for six hours, stirring occasionally. Just before serving, cook noodles according to package directions. Thoroughly mix flour with sour cream, than add to meat mixture, stirring well after each addition. Do not boil after sour cream is added. Serve meat mixture over hot noodles.

Family gathering at Pen's nephew, Bryant's, home in Las Cruces, NM in 2007

Welch Photo Collection

Taco Casserole

Ingredients:

1 lb. burger
1 packet taco seasoning
2 cans ranch style beans
Jalapeno pepper slices, as many as desired
1 lb. cheddar cheese, grated
Tortilla chips

Using a 12" Dutch oven, brown the burger, mixing the taco seasoning with the burger. Layer the seasoned burger in the bottom of the DO. Mix the desired amount of jalapeno slices to the beans and layer on top of the seasoned burger as a layer. Add the cheese as the next layer. Top it off with chips to the top of the DO. Cover and cook for 30 minutes using 8 briquets on the bottom and about 20 on the lid.

Mark Taylor
San Antonio, Texas

Sloppy Joes

Ingredients:

1 lb. hamburger
½ cup chopped onion, optional
1 10 oz. can tomato soup
¼ cup brown sugar
1 Tbsp. molasses
2 tsp. Worcestershire sauce
2 tsp. mustard
Hamburger buns

Brown hamburger and onion. Stir in remaining ingredients and heat through. Serve on buns.

COOKING –
YO ADVENTURE CAMP STYLE

My old pal, Hank Ketchie, wasn't a cowboy, he was a horseman! I've been around a few, and although there may some better, Hank was the best I've ever known. His reasoning was that a mustang was just a blank slate, and training them was easier because he didn't have to undo bad habits condoned by their well-intentioned but uninformed owners.

With years of teaching under my belt, I've come to realize that the same principle applies to teaching Dutch oven cookin'. It's been my pleasure for the last couple of years to teach Dutch oven cookin', along with rope braiding, knot tying, and horse packing at the YO Ranch Adventure Camp. Trust me, when a bunch of kids show up for some Dutch oven cookin' after a week at the YO, bears some semblance to a bunch of mustangs.

With a week of experiencing everything the famous Texas ranch can offer under their belts, these kids remind me of sponges ready to soak up even more. As a teacher, I believe in the principle of "hands-on learnin'"! In a space of four hours, the kids, with just a little help, bake the biscuits, "No Name Creek Baked Beans", the desserts; all to accompany the "Stuffed Back Strap" prepared by the YO cook for their awards dinner at the conclusion of the camp. Young and malleable, hungry kids are the answer to every teacher's prayer.

Besides the DO cookin' I spend a day with the campers showing them how to pack a horse, tie knots, and braid rope. As a teacher, there is nothing more rewarding than seeing kids with big wide eyes exclaiming "Wow!" Such is the case when after showing them how to pack on a Decker Pack Saddle, I can unpack that same horse blindfolded in about a minute. My message to the kids is that if you do the same thing the same way every time, one knows things both backwards and forwards with the reward being consistent results.

Though it's my job to teach the kids, it's amazing how much I learn from them. Though we of the "older generation" often sell the younger generations short, my experience at the YO is that just like a mustang, the uncluttered minds of kids will learn those lessons, skills, and attitudes to keep alive the skills and traditions of us old grey-haired codgers!

Having demonstrated to the kids how to pack a horse, Cee Dub accepts the challenge to unpack the horse in 60 seconds and blindfolded 2008   YO Photo Collection

Cee Dub teaching the YO Adventure Campers all about Dutch oven cookin' 2008   Welch Photo Collection

Delicious YO Stuffed Back Straps on the grill in 2007
Welch Photo Collection

— YO Ranch Stuffed Back Straps —

Ingredients:

Desired number of game back straps
Lime juice
Seasonings, to taste
Cream cheese, softened
Bacon strips

Slice the back straps lengthwise, laying out the back strap as you cut. When you are done, you will have a flat piece of meat about ½ inch thick. The thinner the back straps are cut, the more filling can be applied. With the back straps laid flat, spritz or sprinkle lime juice over the meat. Season the meat. Spread cream cheese over the entire piece of meat. Roll the back straps up like jelly rolls. Lay out bacon strips and place back straps on the strips. Criss-cross strips over and around the back straps and secure with toothpicks. Grill the back straps, turning occasionally, until thoroughly cooked. Slice off pieces about an inch or two long and serve hot.

Eric White
YO Ranch
Mountain Home, Texas

Desserts

— Amy Tanner's Cranberry Sherbet —

Ingredients:

1 lb. cranberrys (4 cups)
2 1/2 cups water
2 cups sugar
Juice of 2 lemons, strained
1 tps. plain Knox gelatin dissolved
        in 1/2 cup cold water

Boil cranberrys in the water until the popping stops. Rub the entire hot mixture (water and berries) through a seive. Add sugar and heat until dissolved. Cool to room temperature. Stir in lemon juice and gelatin water mixture. Pour into container and freeze.

NOTE: No Dutch oven used. According to Jim, this recipe is great for Thanksgiving and Christmas. But, actually good anytime!

Jim Tanner
San Francisco, California

———— Brian's Big Cookie ————

Ingredients:

1 pkg. store-bought cookie dough, or
        homemade equivalent, about 18 oz.

Lightly spray a 12" Dutch oven with vegetable spray. Spread cookie dough evenly throughout the DO. Bake for 25 to 30 minutes, using 6-8 briquets under the DO and 18-22 briquets on the lid. The result is a quick and easy cookie-cake that is also great the next morning.

Brian Welch
Boise, Idaho

── Chocolate Macadamia Pie ──

Ingredients:

½ cup melted butter
1 cup semi-sweet chocolate chips
½ cup plain flour
½ white sugar
½ cup packed brown sugar
2 eggs, beaten
1 tsp. vanilla
½ cup milk chocolate chips
½ cup white chocolate chips
1 cup coarsely chopped macadamia nuts
1 9-10 inch unbaked pie shell

Preheat oven to 350 degrees. In large bowl, combine slightly warmed butter with semi-sweet chips; chips will partially melt. In a separate bowl, mix flour and sugars, then add to chocolate and butter mixture. Add the eggs and vanilla. Stir until combined. Add milk chocolate chips, white chocolate chips, and nuts. Stir and pour into pie shell. Bake until top is brown and crust appears baked, about 45 to 50 minutes. Cool on rack.

Herbs grown in Cee Dub and Pen's garden. Use fresh herbs every chance you get. The flavor they impart to recipes surpasses any store-bought herb in a little bottle.

CILANTRO SLIM

Kerry Rainey of San Angelo, Texas, showed up at our place along the South Fork of Clearwater River in July of 2004 to attend our four-day Dutch Oven University Clinic. I'll never forget the sight of this "long tall Texan" uncoiling out of a little white rental car in our driveway! The first thing he said as he looked at the mountains on all sides was, "Where I come from, you can stand on a tuna fish can and see the whole world!" As tall as Kerry is, that may be possible, but for us folks who may be a bit vertically challenged, we would need to stand on an old ten gallon milk can to see as much of the world as Kerry sees flat footed!

Anyway...over the course of the next four days Kerry jumped right into the Dutch oven cookin' in a big way. Just from watching him work and interact with the other participants, I quickly figured out that Kerry takes his cooking seriously and that he wasn't a total stranger to Dutch ovens. Evenings around the campfire were a special treat for all of us listening to Kerry with his soft West Texas drawl tell of his adventures as a hot air balloon pilot, plus stories of how he became a camp cook.

In our clinics we encourage folks to adapt recipes to suit their own taste. It didn't take long before everyone attending figured out that Kerry REALLY LIKED CILANTRO! It seemed that whenever his group was handed a recipe at the start of a cooking session, Kerry would look up and say, "Would it be OK to add a little cilantro?" If memory serves me correct, by day three we made the fifteen mile trip to town for more cilantro. It was about this time I started calling Kerry "Cilantro Slim" to acknowledge not only his height but his love of cilantro. It stuck!

When Pen and I moved to Texas the fall of 2006, Kerry and his wife, Jamie, showed up for a two-day clinic wearing aprons embroidered with, you guessed it, "Cilantro Slim". Since his retirement Slim and Jamie picked up a chuck wagon and cater out of their home town of San Angelo, Texas. If you get a chance, visit their website, www.cilantroslim.com

Slim and Jamie's "go-to" dessert for their catering business is a peach and apricot cobbler which they graciously shared with Pen and me. They use the pastry crust from our blackberry cobbler recipe in More Cee Dub's Dutch Oven & Other Camp Cookin', and their own fruit mixture with a special ingredient which adds a very distinctive flavor!

The VERY TALL GUY in the picture is Kerry, aka Cilantro Slim, and Jamie, his wife, is standing in front. Taken at Hunt DO Clinic November 2006   B Truitt Photo

Words of Wisdom

When putting together a camp kitchen, first determine exactly what is essential to your style of cooking and the recipes you prepare. To economize on space and weight, select items that nest together, have a dual purpose, and are non-breakable. If you don't need it, don't pack it!

— Cilantro Slim's Peach Cobbler —

Pastry Ingredients:

2 cups unbleached flour
2 sticks butter
6 oz. cream cheese
Pinch of salt

Filling Ingredients:

4 cups fresh peaches, cut in wedges
2 cups fresh apricots, cut in halves
1 cup pineapple chunks, optional
1 cup flour
½ cup sugar or honey
½ tsp. nutmeg
1 tsp. cinnamon
2 Tbsp. melted butter or margarine
1 tsp. lemon or lime juice
¼ cup Amaretto

Pastry:

Soften the butter and cream cheese at room temperature for about an hour. Cut into the flour to which you have added the pinch of salt. Work the dough into a ball and place in the fridge or cooler for a couple of hours, placing in a large resealable bag or wrap in plastic wrap. Note: when cooking for large groups, the crusts can be made a day ahead of time. Crust can be frozen.

Filling:

Mix fruit in a 12" Dutch oven. Sprinkle flour over fruit for a thickener; then add sugar or honey. Dust with nutmeg and cinnamon. Drizzle with melted butter, lemon or lime juice, and Amaretto.

Roll crust out on a floured cutting board to approximately 11 inches in diameter. Place over filling and sprinkle with a bit of cinnamon or nutmeg for color. Bake with

6-8 briquets underneath and 18-22 on top for about 50 minutes, or bake uncovered in the oven at 375 degrees for about 50 minutes or until crust is golden brown. Allow to cool and serve with good vanilla ice cream. In Texas, make sure it's Blue Bell!

Kerry Rainey aka "Cilantro Slim"
San Angelo, Texas

—— Jill's French Vanilla Ice Cream ——

Ingredients:

8 eggs, beaten
2 cups sugar
2 4 oz. packages French vanilla instant pudding
½ tsp. salt
2 Tbsp. pure vanilla
1 pt. whipping cream
1 qt. half and half
Milk

Mix together eggs and sugar. Add instant pudding and mix until smooth. Add salt, vanilla, whipping cream, and half and half. Mix thoroughly. Put mixture in ice cream maker, add milk to fill, and cover. Add ice and ice cream salt around canister. Churn until firm. If using a Dutch oven to make ice cream, put mixture in a 12 inch aluminum Dutch oven. Put lid on DO. Put ice and ice cream salt in a cooler. Put DO in ice and salt mixture. Using the bale, twist DO back and forth. Occasionally take lid off and stir with a spoon. Continue to mix until ice cream sets up. NOTE: This recipe contains raw eggs.

Jill stated that adding a package of vanilla bean sugar, 1 cup of fresh berries such as raspberries, strawberries, or blueberries, are great additions. She also likes to make this recipe using white chocolate instant pudding mix.

Jill Varin
Castleford, Idaho

Coca-Cola Cake

Ingredients:

2 cups flour
2 cups sugar
1 cup butter
3 Tbsp. cocoa
1 cup Coca-Cola
1 tsp. baking Soda
½ cup buttermilk
2 eggs, beaten
1 tsp. vanilla
2 cups miniature marshmallows

Preheat oven to 350 degrees. If using a12" Dutch oven,
preheat the lid using 20-22 briquets on the lid. Combine
flour and sugar in a bowl. Melt butter in a saucepan; add
cocoa and Coca-Cola. Heat until just boiling. Cool slightly.
Pour over flour mixture. Stir until blended. Dissolve baking
soda in buttermilk; gradually add to flour mixture with
eggs and vanilla. Mix well. Stir in marshmallows and pour
into a greased and floured 9" x 13" pan or a greased
and floured 12" Dutch oven. Batter will be thin and
marshmallows will come to the top. Bake 40 to 45 minutes
uncovered in the oven; or, put loaded lid on the DO and
bake with 6-8 briquets under the DO. Ice while cake is hot.

Icing:

½ cup butter
3 Tbsp. cocoa
6 Tbsp. Coca-Cola
1 pound powered sugar
1 tsp. vanilla
1 cup nuts, chopped

Combine butter, cocoa, and Coca-Cola in a saucepan.
Heat until boiling. Put sugar in electric mixer bowl and
pour butter mixture over sugar. Beat until smooth. Add
vanilla. Stir in nuts and set aside.

— Dwain's Cherry Pecan Cobbler —

Ingredients:

There's nothing "lite" about this recipe! But if you want a deliciously rich and decadent dessert, try this one. We often serve this cobbler to top off a special dinner for guests at the ranch. It is always a big hit. Don't forget the ice cream!

Ingredients:

2 sticks butter, divided
2 cans cherry pie filling
1 Duncan Hines™ French Vanilla cake mix
½ cup brown sugar
1 cup chopped pecans, more or less as desired

Melt three quarters of a stick of butter in a small frying pan. While maintaining a very low temperature, add brown sugar and pecans, a tablespoon or so at a time, and stir into butter. Continue to heat on low temperature until sugar is nearly dissolved. Do not over cook or mixture will harden. Set aside. Melt one-quarter stick butter in the bottom of a 10 inch Dutch oven. Melt another stick of butter and set aside. Add the pie filling to butter in the DO. Sprinkle on cake mix and level. Drizzle the one stick of melted butter over the cake mix. Spoon the pecan mix on top. Cover and bake 50 to 60 minutes using 4-6 briquets under the DO and 13-15 on the lid. Serve with Blue Bell™ vanilla ice cream. NOTE: Cherry pie filling and vanilla flavored cake mix are Dwain's favorites for this recipe, but other flavors of fruit pie filling and cake mix can be used.

Dwain Riney
Las Piedras Ranch
Real County, Texas

GUY'S SOURDOUGH CAKE

One Monday morning after a 4th of July weekend, we got an email from our pal, Guy Perkins. He is a great DO cook and is always coming up with entertaining stories about his hunting and cooking adventures and new great recipes. This email just goes to show you how creative he can be! It read as follows:

Man this was a good cake. I used the Cee Dub method of measuring...or, "How does that feel to ya!"

I started by using my sourdough for pancakes in the am. Made about a dozen, and left the rest of the sponge while I figured out what I wanted to do with it. We were having all the family including my mom and brother's crew over. So I ventured out to the freezer to see if perhaps there were some frozen berries to fill up my Camp Chef DO-14; and glory be, there were 6 cups of South Fork Blackberries I'd picked at Cee Dub's! I put em in a glass measuring cup and added about 1/2 cup of sugar to the top. After an hour of thawing I gave em a stir just to get the sugar around town. About another hour into it, I added two packets of original instant oatmeal. I gave em another stir and let em rest.

I could have went to a recipe book to get the cake right, by someone else's standards, but hey...what kind of adventure would that have been? Iwhisked up three eggs, added them and about 1/2 cup of sugar to the sourdough sponge from am. Then maybe two cups of flour, three tablespoons of soda to the two cupishes of sponge with a shot of milk (cupish). Then went to whipping with a wooden spoon. The sponge looked good and active with the right consistency (like a cake mix out of a box). For laughs I added two twitches of vanilla (two tablespoons). (No, I didn't miss it...I didn't use any oil!)

I wiped the dutch oven's inside walls and bottom with a little oil. Then I poured what looked to be half of the batter in the bottom. I scattered the berries next, then

Guy with his fall 2008 turkey   Perkins Photo Collection

covered them with the remaining batter. It was a hot day, about 92f outside, so I set 8 charcoals under the bottom in circular fashion just under the outside edge of the oven and put twenty on top. I wish I could tell you exactly how long it cooked…but I can't! I was busy cooking venison bacon burgers when I smelled it being finished. I'd guess I was and hour into it, anyway, cause the charcoal was burned down by half.

Can't seem to get a good name to come to me… maybe I should call it "gone away blackberry sourdough cake" cause that is what it did! The pot was all but licked clean!

You can name it and toss it in the new cookbook if you want.

Best,

Guy

Easy Apple Crisp

Ingredients:

1 cup cornbread mix
½ cup flour
1 ¼ cups brown sugar, divided
¼ cup white sugar
½ tsp. baking powder
3/4 tsp. cinnamon, divided
Pinch of salt
1 egg
1 stick butter, softened
¼ cup dried cranberries
¼ cup cinnamon red hots,
1 tsp. grated lemon zest or juice
2-3 apples, sliced

Combine cornbread mix, flour, ¾ cup brown sugar, white sugar, baking powder, ¼ teaspoon cinnamon, salt, egg, and butter in a bowl; using a pastry cutter or working with your fingers. Texture should be crumbly. Set aside. In a small bowl, mix together ½ teaspoon cinnamon, dried cranberries, red hots, ½ cup brown sugar, and lemon zest. Set aside. Fill a 9 inch pie pan about half full of sliced apples. If using lemon juice, sprinkle over apples. Sprinkle dried cranberry and red hot mix over apples. Cover with crisp topping mix. Bake until bubbling and apples are soft when poked with a fork.

Hobart Manns
Portland, Oregon

Words of Wisdom

Apples are easier to peel if you first cut them into quarters.

When baking apple pies, consider grating the apples instead of slicing them into wedges; it saves time.

Alec and Anna getting a baking lesson 2008
Welch Photo Collection

Light Tiramisu

Ingredients:

1 prepared 8 inch angel food cake,
   cut into 1 inch cubes
½ cup instant sugar-free cappuccino mix, divided
2 cups cold fat-free milk, divided
1 8 oz. package fat-free cream cheese, softened
1 1oz. package sugar-free instant
   vanilla pudding mix
2 cups reduced-fat whipped topping
½ tsp. baking cocoa

Place cake cubes in an ungreased 13 x 9 inch dish or
12 inch Dutch oven. In a small bowl, combine ¼ cup
cappuccino mix and ½ cup milk until dissolved. Pour over
cake. In mixing bowl, beat cream cheese. In another bowl,
combine pudding mix, remaining cappuccino mix, and
milk; whisk until smooth and thick. Add to cream cheese
and mix well. Fold in whipped topping; then spoon over
cake mixture. Refrigerate for at least 3 hours. Sprinkle with
cocoa just before serving. Serves 8.

THE GIFT

We are always trying to give Dwain Riney gifts for Christmas that are somewhat unique. We decided to give him a Lodge baby Dutch oven, a collector's item. But to make it a special surprise, we came up with the idea of baking the Dutch oven into a loaf of bread baked in another, much larger, Dutch oven. At Riney's house before dinner, Butch turned the loaf out, containing the baby Dutch, onto the butcher block and handed Dwain a bread knife to do the honors of cutting the bread. Boy, was he ever surprised! Well, one thing led to another, and we decided to bake one of Dwain's favorites, Bread Pudding. But for an extra treat, we baked the Whiskey Sauce in the baby Dutch inside the bread pudding. We sprinnkled a few cranberries on top for color. It was very appetizing!

Cee Dub's *Las Piedras* Bread Pudding

Ingredients:

3 cups crumbled yeast rolls
3 cups crumbled baking powder biscuits
3 cups milk or half and half
3 eggs
½ cup white Karo™ syrup
½ cup sugar
½ tsp. salt
1 tsp. vanilla
¼ tsp. cinnamon
¼ tsp. nutmeg
½ cup raisins, optional

Mix crumbled rolls and biscuits into a 12 inch Dutch oven. In a bowl, thoroughly mix remaining ingredients with a wire whisk and pour over crumbled bread. Add a little additional milk if the bread does not completely soak up the liquid. Bake with 5-7 briquets under the oven and 18-22 on top for 45 to 55 minutes until top is slightly browned. Serve warm with Whiskey Sauce drizzled over the top. Serves 8 to 10.

Welch Photo

———— Pen's Whiskey Sauce ————

Ingredients:

1 cup powdered sugar
1 cup white Karo™ syrup
3 Tbsp. butter
1 tsp. vanilla
1/3 cup whiskey or bourbon

Mix powdered sugar, syrup, and butter in a small saucepan. Heat slowly until boiling. Continue to boil, stirring constantly, until dissolved and smooth. Add vanilla and whiskey; bring back to a boil. Take off heat and set aside. Serve warm, drizzled over bread pudding.

Penny Welch
Mountain Home, Texas

213

Dutches in a firepan showing how to arrange charcoal briquets for baking at Ranch Clinic 2008 Fant Steele Photo

Maple Frosting

Ingredients:

1 cup powdered sugar
1 Tbsp. margarine
½ tsp. Mapleine™ imitation maple flavoring
1 Tbsp. milk

In a small bowl, cut margarine into powdered sugar with a fork. Add maple flavoring and milk; mix thoroughly until creamy. If too thick, mix in a few drops more milk. If too thin, mix in a little more powdered sugar. Spread on slightly cooled maple bars or donuts.

Herb Good
Hood River, Oregon

NOTES: To make vanilla frosting, substitute vanilla for Mapleine™. To make chocolate frosting, leave out the Mapleine™, and add 1 tablespoon cocoa and 1 teaspoon vanilla.

—— No-Bake Boston Cream Cake ——

Ingredients:

1 ½ cups cold half and half
1 package instant vanilla pudding mix
1 loaf frozen pound cake, thawed
¾ cup powdered sugar
2 Tbsp. cocoa
4 tsp. hot water

In a bowl, whisk together cream and pudding mix. Let stand for 5 minutes. Split cake into three horizontal layers. Place bottom layer on a serving plate and top with half of the pudding. Repeat layers and top with the third cake layer. In a small bowl, combine the powdered sugar, cocoa, and hot water to reach a spreading consistency. Spread over top of cake, letting glaze drizzle down sides. Serves 4 to 6.

—— Tomato Cobbler ——

Ingredients:

1 gallon whole tomatoes, chopped
2 large handfuls brown sugar
1 cup dark Karo™ syrup
½ cup white vinegar
2 pie crusts

Cook tomatoes, brown sugar, syrup, and vinegar until liquid is reduced down. Pour one half the tomato mixture a 12" Dutch oven. Cover with one pie crust. Pour remaining tomato mixture on top of crust. Place second pie crust on top. Cover and bake for 45 to 55 minutes at 350 degrees, until golden brown, using 6-8 briquets under the DO and 18-22 on the lid. Bake uncovered if using a home oven.

Lisa Wade
Georgetown, Texas

Pumpkin Dump Cake **

Ingredients:

1 29 oz. can pure pumpkin
1 12 oz. can evaporated milk
3 eggs
1 cup sugar
1 tsp. salt
3 tsp. cinnamon
1 yellow cake mix
1 cup chopped pecans
¾ cup melted butter or margarine

Preheat 12" Dutch oven lid or oven to 350 degrees. Mix pumpkin, milk, eggs, sugar, salt, and cinnamon until well blended. Pour into DO or 9 x 13 inch greased pan. Sprinkle cake mix on top. Cover with pecans. Drizzle melted butter or margarine over. Bake for about 50 minutes uncovered in the oven or using 6-8 briquets under the DO and 18-22 briquets on the lid. Serve with whipped cream or ice cream.

** A photo of this recipe is featured at the beginning of the "Desserts" section.

Brian, Wyatt, and Grandma Penny enjoying Thanksgiving dinner 2007   Welch Photo Collection

Matt & Trina with new arrival, Maggie, 2008
Welch Photo Collection

—— Raspberry Lemon Dump Cake ——

While Matt was in pilot training in Mississippi, Matt and Trina were living in base housing. They had taken their Dutch oven equipment with them from Idaho so that they could cook in the event of a hurricane. They quickly learned, as many people do, that firing up a Dutch oven can attract inquisitive noses and inquiring minds which can lead to many new friends. This dump cake combination became a favorite to make for backyard get-togethers.

Ingredients:

2 cans raspberry pie filling
1 lemon cake mix
1 can 7-Up™ or Sprite™

Put fruit in the bottom of a 12" Dutch oven. Sprinkle the dry cake mix over the fruit and level out, if necessary. Gently pour soda over the cake mix. Cover and bake using 6-8 briquets under the DO and 18-22 on the lid. Baking should take about 45 to 50 minutes. If desired, serve with ice cream.

Matt and Trina Dykas
Boise, Idaho

217

S'mores Bars

Ingredients:

3/4 cup butter
2/3 cup sugar
1 egg
1 tsp. vanilla
18 whole graham crackers, crushed, about 3 cups
1/2 cup all-purpose flour
1/2 tsp. salt
8 milk chocolate bars, approximately
    1 1/2 ounces each
3 1/2 cups miniature marshmallow

Preheat oven to 350 degrees or 12" Dutch oven lid using 18-22 briquets on the lid. Beat butter and sugar with electric mixer on medium speed until light and fluffy. Beat in egg and vanilla. Stir in crushed graham crackers, flour, and salt. Reserve 2 1/2 cups of the graham cracker mixture. Press remaining mixture over the bottom of a greased 13 x 9 inch baking pan or 12" DO. Arrange chocolate bars, in a single layer, over graham cracker mixture in the pan. Sprinkle with marshmallows. Crumble reserved 2 1/2 cups graham cracker mixture over the marshmallows. Cover DO with preheated lid and use 6-8 briquets under DO. Bake for 25 to 30 minutes or until golden brown. Cool in pan or DO for 10 minutes. Cut into bars and cool completely. Makes about 2 dozen bars.

Carol Hampton
Bonners Ferry, Idaho

Words of Wisdom

When going camping, always throw in an extra small plastic tarp. Before going to bed, make sure your firewood pile is covered just in case a storm comes up unexpectedly

218

Swedish Nut Cake

Ingredients:

2 cups sugar
2 cups flour
2 eggs
½ tsp. baking soda
1 20 oz. can crushed pineapple
1 cup chopped walnuts or pecans, divided
1 cup brown sugar
½ stick butter or margarine
8 oz. cream cheese

Preheat oven to 350 degrees, or preheat lid of 12" Dutch oven using 18-22 briquets on the lid. In a large bowl mix sugar, flour, eggs, baking soda, and pineapple with juice. Add one-half cup nuts and pour into 9 x 13 inch greased basking pan or 12" Dutch oven. Put preheated lid on DO and bake for about 40 minutes. Bring butter or margarine to room temperature. For frosting, mix brown sugar, butter or margarine, and cream cheese in a bowl. Spread on cake while it is warm. Sprinkle remaining nuts on top.

Good eatin' with Cee Dub   Welch Photo Collection

PUBLISHER'S NOTE

When we finish a new cookbook we feel a great sense of accomplishment. Each cookbook represents a culmination of our activities and acquaintances over time. Of course, my involvement as the publisher comes more heavily toward the end of each project. We always think we are "done" when we have the first copies of a new cookbook off the press. But is seems that instinctively we start collecting ideas, photos, and recipes for another cookbook. As we travel the country, we continue to be in awe of and humbled by how many people have been inspired by Cee Dub's television shows and his cookbooks. As such, we hope you will enjoy the results of this newest cookbook.

Again, I want to thank Dee Pogue and the rest of the Pogue family for the continued use of the likeness of one of Bill Pogue's prints as the logo for Back Country Press. It represents many meaningful things in our lives.

Penny L. Welch
Back Country Press

NOTES

NOTES